MOBILIZING CAPITAL FOR LOCAL GOVERNMENT FINANCE IN ASIA AND THE PACIFIC THROUGH GREEN, SOCIAL, AND SUSTAINABILITY BOND MARKETS

DECEMBER 2025

ASIAN DEVELOPMENT BANK

ADB

6 ADB Avenue, Mandaluyong City, 1550 Metro Manila, Philippines
Tel +63 2 8632 4444; Fax +63 2 8636 2444
www.adb.org

ISBN 978-92-9277-561-2 (print); 978-92-9277-562-9 (PDF); 978-92-9277-563-6 (e-book)
Publication Stock No. TCS250513-2
DOI: http://dx.doi.org/10.22617/TCS250513-2

Corrigenda to ADB publications may be found at http://www.adb.org/publications/corrigenda.

Note:
In this publication, ADB recognizes "China" as the People's Republic of China, "$" refers to United States dollars, "€" refers to euros, "¥" refers to yen, "R" refers to South African rand, "SKr" refers to Swedish kronor.

Cover design by Erickson Mercado.

CONTENTS

continued on next page

FIGURES, TABLES, AND BOXES

FIGURES

TABLES

continued on next page

Tables: continued

BOXES

ACKNOWLEDGMENTS

This report is a knowledge product developed by the Asian Development Bank (ADB) through its regional technical assistance under the Asian Bond Markets Initiative, financially supported by the People's Republic of China (PRC) Poverty Reduction and Regional Cooperation Fund as well as the Green Climate Fund (GCF), and the United Kingdom through their contributions to ASEAN Catalytic Green Finance Facility (ACGF).

This report was a collaborative effort led by Kosintr Puongsophol (senior financial sector specialist, Economic Research and Development Impact Department [ERDI], ADB) and Jason Mortimer (head of sustainable development–fixed income and senior portfolio manager, Nomura Asset Management), with significant contributions from Deeny Simanjuntak (principal project officer, Indonesia Resident Mission, ADB); Pitchaya Sirivunnabood (consultant, Southeast Asia Department [SERD], ADB); Fonthip Yuthaseree (consultant, ERDI, ADB); Chi Xiang Wong (consultant, ERDI, ADB); and the PwC Luxembourg consulting team led by Tsvetelina Blagoeva (director). Overall production coordination of the report was managed by Richard Supangan (principal economic officer, ERDI, ADB), Oth Marulou M. Gagni (senior operations assistant, ERDI, ADB), Vincent Joshua D. Inola (operations assistant, ERDI, ADB), and Alita Lestor, consultant, ERDI, ADB). Editing was done by Kevin Donahue (consultant, ERDI, ADB), proofreading by Lawrence Casiraya.

Special recognition goes to ADB staff members Christine Engstrom (director-general, SD3); Scott Roberts (head of the Green Finance Hub Unit, SERD); Anouj Mehta (country director, Thailand Resident Mission); Jennifer Romero-Torres (principal sustainable finance specialist, SD3); and Sree Kartha (consultant, SERD, ADB) for their guidance and advice in developing this report.

The report draws on research and analysis from ADB consultants and the PwC consulting team. The design and layout were done by Erickson Mercado (consultant, ERDI, ADB).

KEY FINDINGS

Cities are at the forefront of global population growth, economic activity, and energy consumption. They are also the most significant contributors to greenhouse gas emissions and highly exposed to climate-related risks, making them key centers for climate action. Local governments are therefore pivotal actors in financing and delivering sustainable infrastructure projects that address the environmental and social challenges in their communities. Their proximity to and understanding of local conditions makes them uniquely positioned to align investments with specific local mitigation and adaptation needs.

However, many challenges remain. Local governments are often constrained by limited resources and institutional capacity, particularly for finance-raising through capital markets. Borrowing limits and credit rating requirements further restrict their access to financing, while a lack of technical expertise hampers the development of eligible project pipelines. Despite these hurdles, many local governments have found success in tapping capital markets for sustainable finance, either issuing bonds directly to the market or through local government financing organizations that pool issuer resources and borrowing needs. Local government borrowers around the world now regularly issue green, social, sustainability, sustainability-linked, and other labeled (GSS+) bonds to highlight their commitment to sustainable development and attract long-term financing from investors for high-impact infrastructure projects.

This report analyzes the structure of local government bond markets globally; reviews sub-sovereign financing (including the use of municipal financing organizations); and assesses the advantages of funding local sustainable infrastructure with GSS+ bonds. It provides examples of commonly used green and sustainable use of proceeds, and case studies from municipal borrowers issuing GSS+ bonds to finance local mitigation, adaptation, and resilience projects.

The following are the key takeaways from this report:

1. Local Government Borrowers Increasingly Use GSS+ Bonds for Financing

    - Local governments increasingly use GSS+ bonds to secure long-term financing for sustainable infrastructure and municipal service delivery. These sustainable finance instruments can help local issuers diversify their revenue sources and offset declining fiscal allocations from central governments. They also provide community-based investment opportunities for local investors and promote capital market deepening.

    - GSS+ bonds now account for over 10% of local government issuance annually in several advanced economies, including Australia, Japan, the Netherlands, and Sweden—demonstrating the format's suitability to local borrowers in a variety of contexts. Cities in developing economies such as India, South Africa, and Türkiye have also issued GSS+ local government bonds.

    - GSS+ bonds can deliver long-term, competitively priced capital to local borrowers by aligning public sector needs with private investor demand for high-impact, sustainable finance opportunities.

2. GSS+ Bonds Finance a Range of Local Mitigation, Adaptation, and Resilience Projects

   - Local government borrowing and infrastructure development needs are well served by the GSS+ bond format, which is specifically designed to finance mitigation, adaptation, and resilience projects. This publication explores the range of eligible use-of-proceeds bond projects most relevant to municipal and local government borrowers, including

     - **mitigation:** sustainable water and sewer infrastructure, clean mass transit, clean energy installation and generation promotion, green public buildings, energy efficiency retrofitting for municipal facilities, and local environmental preservation such as parks and green space development; and

     - **adaptation and resilience:** infrastructure for flood and stormwater management (levees, seawalls, permeable pavements); measures for drought and water stress resilience (waterworks efficiency, leak detection and management); measures for heat-resilience (urban cooling centers and green corridors); climate-smart public buildings (flood-proofing and elevated public buildings); and nature-based solutions (wetland and mangrove restoration and shoreline stabilization).

   - GSS+ financing frameworks can be tailored to reflect the unique circumstances and strategic priorities of different local government borrowers. For example, the city of Cape Town issued a green bond to fund water infrastructure and climate mitigation projects in response to acute drought conditions. The Tokyo Metropolitan Government has issued GSS+ bonds to finance mitigation, adaptation, and physical resilience initiatives aligned with the city's strategic environmental and social goals.

3. Local Government Borrowers Can Pool Resources with Municipal Finance Organizations

   - Local governments often lack the scale and capacity to access capital markets and issue bonds independently. By pooling resources and project financing into jointly established financing vehicles, smaller local borrowers can enhance access to capital markets by aggregating their creditworthiness and issuance volumes. These vehicles, also known as municipal finance organizations, can improve borrowing terms for their members by tapping a wider range of long-term institutional capital, reducing overhead and administration costs through economies of scale, and developing high-quality sustainable financing frameworks for issuing GSS+ bonds.

   - Municipal finance organizations are well established in the Nordic region, with several institutions now over 100 years old. New examples have been launched recently in France and the United Kingdom. In Asia and the Pacific, Japan has one of the world's largest local government bond markets that includes both a specific debt instrument issued directly by local governments, known as Joint Local Government Bonds, and a dedicated municipal finance institution, the Japan Finance Organization for Municipalities.

   - The Japan Finance Organization for Municipalities was established to provide long-term and low-cost funding to local government projects essential to citizen's daily lives such as sewerage, water supply, hospitals, and local public transportation. Reflecting this mandate, the organization issued its first green bond in 2020 with a framework specifically focused on sustainable water and wastewater management projects. Today, it regularly issues green bonds in international and domestic markets.

4. Development Partners Can Help Catalyze Local Government GSS+ Issuance Programs

- Development partners like the Asian Development Bank can play a catalytic role in supporting subnational governments and municipalities to overcome key challenges to accessing sustainable finance. This includes helping to build institutional capacity, developing pipelines of eligible projects, and structuring green and sustainable finance frameworks that align with national frameworks and priorities. Such support is essential to facilitate the issuance of GSS+ municipal bonds, enabling local governments to mobilize long-term capital for climate-aligned and socially inclusive infrastructure.

- To crowd in private capital and reduce funding costs for local governments, development partners can offer financial support mechanisms such as guarantees, risk-sharing facilities, and concessional loans. Platforms like the Catalytic Green Finance Facility of the Association of Southeast Asian Nations (ASEAN) can help kickstart local government bond market development by overcoming common barriers—such as a lack of bankable, climate-aligned project pipelines and credit ratings—and by providing support to address institutional capacity limitations.

- Local governments can benefit from technical assistance for developing green and social financing frameworks that align with relevant national taxonomies, which serve as reference tools for identifying eligible projects. Development partners can also facilitate the preparation of sustainability disclosures, deepen communication and engagement with investors, and promote regulatory dialogue to ensure sound governance and market integrity.

1. INTRODUCTION

Local governments play a vital role in delivering municipal infrastructure and services that directly shape community living standards. These investments provide a resilient foundation for economic growth through improvements in transportation, water management, health care, education, housing, and disaster risk management (including early warning systems).[1] As a key enabler of sustainable development, subnational governments contribute to the achievement of roughly 65% of the 169 targets underpinning the 17 global Sustainable Development Goals.[2]

The importance of local government investment is especially pronounced in Asia and the Pacific, a region characterized by densely populated megacities, significant municipal infrastructure development needs, rapid urbanization, widening inequality, and heightened vulnerability to climate and disaster risks. Although governance structures vary across the region, local governments are often best suited to respond to these challenges through locally tailored solutions.

With the right enabling policies, green, social, sustainability, sustainability-linked, and other labeled (GSS+) bonds can provide local governments with an effective mechanism to mobilize long-term capital for sustainable infrastructure projects. These sustainable financing instruments are now a mainstream product for global fixed-income investors and are well suited to financing projects that deliver tangible social and environmental benefits to communities, aligning local action with global goals.

This Asian Development Bank knowledge product aims to inform and motivate policymakers and local governments to explore practical approaches for developing and integrating environmental and social elements into project design and development. By embedding these elements early in the planning process, borrowers can effectively identify and develop eligible projects for funding through thematic GSS+ local government bonds.

The report analyzes the structure of global local bond markets; outlines the development of sub-sovereign financing, including the use of municipal financing organizations; and assesses the relevance and advantages of GSS+ bonds in financing local sustainable infrastructure, with example use-of-proceeds categories for mitigation, adaptation, and resilience projects.

To illustrate practical applications, the report presents case studies from Japan, France, South Africa, and Sweden, showcasing how local governments have successfully grown local debt capital markets for GSS+ bonds to deliver sustainable public infrastructure that meets local needs, with discussion and analysis of issuer motivation, frameworks, use of proceeds, and lessons learned. The report concludes with policy recommendations for developing GSS+ bond markets for local government borrowers.

1 "Local government" refers to all forms of subnational government including those at the regional, state, municipal, and local level.

2 Organisation for Economic Co-operation and Development (OECD). 2020. A Territorial Approach to the Sustainable Development Goals: Synthesis Report. *OECD Urban Policy Reviews.* https://doi.org/10.1787/e86fa715-en.

2. EMPOWERING LOCAL GOVERNMENTS TO FINANCE SUSTAINABLE DEVELOPMENT

2.1 Local Governments Are Key Players in Sustainable Development

Cities are at the forefront of population growth, economic output, energy consumption, and exposure to physical risks. They hold 56% of the world's population, generate over 80% of global gross domestic product (GDP), account for 70% of energy use, and produce 75% of greenhouse gas (GHG) emissions, making them a high-impact domain for climate action.[3] They play a direct role in decarbonization efforts, with primary responsibility for as much as 28% of total nonenergy global GHG abatement potential by 2050.[4]

At the same time, cities also face elevated physical climate risks due to dense populations and concentrated economic activity, making urban climate adaptation projects highly cost-effective and impactful. Intensifying climate hazards—such as flooding, water stress, and heat waves—threaten local communities and municipal infrastructure, necessitating a holistic approach to improving resilience. While national climate policies often focus on nationwide strategies for high-level resource deployment, subnational and municipal governments possess local insights that enable them to identify specific local infrastructure needs and efficiently coordinate implementation for maximum impact.

2.2 How Local Governments Finance Sustainable Development Infrastructure Projects

Local government authorities are responsible for delivering essential municipal services and public infrastructure within their jurisdictions. Their proximity to residents makes them well attuned to local development needs and well positioned to design context-specific solutions.

In some cases, local governments can self-finance smaller projects using own-source revenues such as local taxes, user fees, or accumulated capital reserves. However, their capacity to mobilize sufficient long-term capital for large-scale investments is often constrained by a limited local tax base, stagnant or unpredictable intergovernmental transfers, and fiscal rules that restrict local borrowing or deficit financing. Combined with a general reluctance to incur debt among fiscally conservative local governments, this often leads to underinvestment in public infrastructure.

To address these constraints, local governments may seek external financing for long-term investment projects through public–private partnerships (PPPs) or by borrowing from financial institutions and investors, including through the issuance of municipal or local government bonds. The funding for debt servicing and project maintenance typically comes from revenue sources such as local taxes, user charges or tariffs, earmarked revenues, or intergovernmental capital transfers and grants.

---

3 World Bank. 2023. *Urban Development Overview.* https://www.worldbank.org/en/topic/urbandevelopment/overview; International Energy Agency. 2024. Executive Summary of *Empowering Urban Energy Transitions.* https://www.iea.org/reports/empoweringurban-energy-transitions/executive-summary.

4 Coalition for Urban Transitions. 2019. *Climate Emergency, Urban Opportunity: How National Governments Can Secure Economic Prosperity and Avert Climate Catastrophe by Transforming Cities.* World Resources Institute Ross Centre for Sustainable Cities.

2.3 Bridging the Financing Gap for Local Governments in Developing Economies

Estimates of spending needs for low-carbon and climate-resilient urban infrastructure in emerging markets range from $2.5 trillion to $4.0 trillion, with over $200 billion needed for adaptation alone (**Figure 1**). Much of this spending is in Asia and the Pacific, a region highly vulnerable to climate impacts and home to many rapidly urbanizing economies. However, total estimated flows to urban climate finance worldwide reached only $831 billion in 2021/22, including $407 billion in Asia and the Pacific, with nearly all of these funds allocated to mitigation projects (e.g., clean transport and green buildings) and very little to adaptation.[5]

This stark imbalance underscores the urgent need for local governments to develop new and additional sources of climate finance, particularly for adaptation, amid constrained central government fiscal resources and borrowing capacity.

Figure 1: Global Adaptation Financing to Emerging Markets and Developing Economies—Annual Flows and Projected Needs

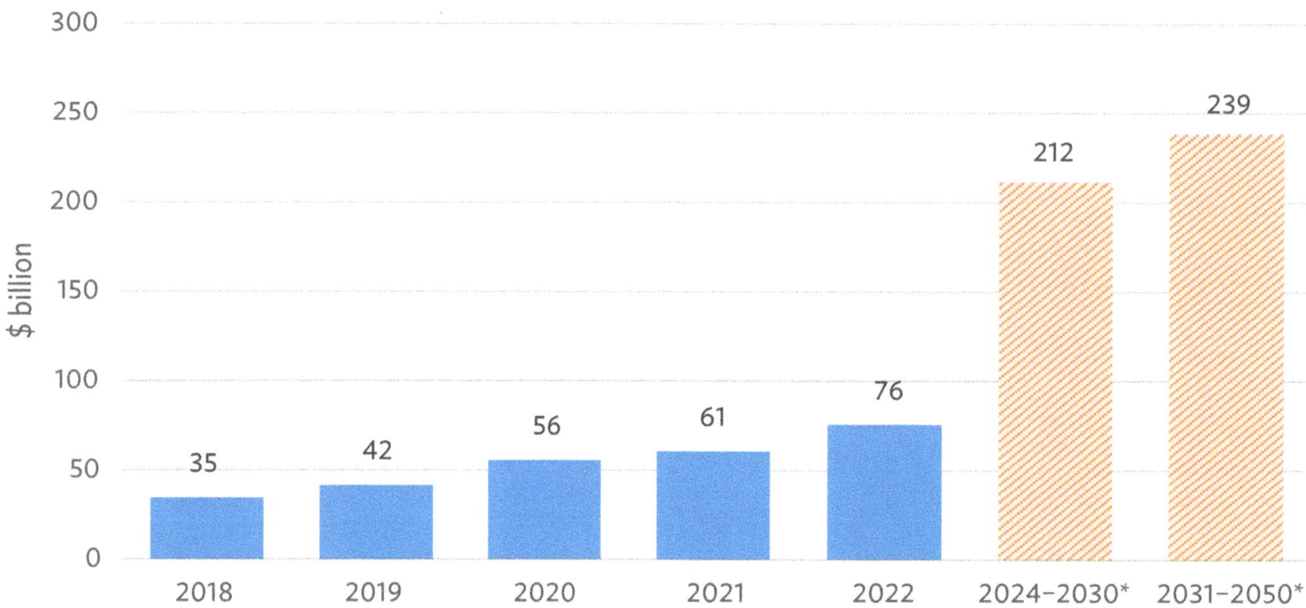

* = projected values.

Notes: Projected needs are annual averages. Figures are likely underestimates as they only account for the needs of emerging markets and developing economies (EMDEs), and many costs cannot be accurately measured. From 2018 to 2022, EMDEs accounted for 92% of adaptation finance flows.

Source: B. Naran et al. 2024. Global Landscape of Climate Finance 2024. Climate Policy Initiative.

2.4 Building Local Government Bond Markets: Policy and Capacity Foundations

Direct bond issuance by local governments can help address these financing gaps. However, establishing a local government bond market requires both central government policy support and local institutional capacity building. Central governments play a critical role by developing policies and regulatory oversight to foster the development of subnational debt markets and enable local government entities to finance sustainable infrastructure effectively.[6]

---

[5] Cities Climate Finance Leadership Alliance. 2024. *The State of Cities Climate Finance 2024*. https://citiesclimatefinance.org/publications/2024-state-of-cities-climate-finance

[6] OECD. 2022. 2022 *Synthesis Report World Observatory on Subnational Government Finance and Investment*. https://doi.org/10.1787/b80a8cdb-en.

This process begins with creating an appropriate legal framework that authorizes local governments to raise funds responsibly. It also includes regulations governing the approval and use of debt financing, legal mechanisms for resolving defaults, disclosure requirements for local government issuers, and prudential borrowing limits to address the risk of moral hazard and opaque or pro-cyclical borrowing.[7]

Because sound repayment structures are essential for attracting investors to finance local government projects, central governments should ensure that local authorities have access to reliable fiscal resources to service interest and principal payments on long-term borrowings. This can be supported through reforms to local tax allocations and diversification of revenue sources, including those from infrastructure use, and/or the reallocation of central government revenues.[8]

For local government borrowers, successful bond issuance depends on effective planning, preparation, and follow-through. These functions are also essential for the healthy development of local government bond markets for investors.

For capital planning, local issuing authorities must identify current and future infrastructure and service delivery needs, taking into consideration economic and demographic trends as well as climate and physical risk mitigation needs. These assessments inform the size, tenor, and schedule of local government bond issuance, which is essential for investors who prefer regular, predictable issuance programs with larger, more liquid benchmark bonds that can be consistently covered by credit analysts. A national integrated sustainable financing framework can promote policy coherence between local and central governments and help to identify high-priority, high-impact investment projects at the local level to mobilize private climate finance.[9]

For issuance preparation and follow-through, prospective local government issuers need to develop adequate capacities for auditing, accounting, and asset–liability risk management.[10] They should also seek to obtain a credit rating from a registered credit rating agency and establish an investor relations function for ongoing market outreach and public reporting.[11]

2.5 GSS+ Bonds: A Strategic Tool for Local Sustainable Finance

With a suitable policy framework in place and backed by robust budgetary, accounting, and financial risk management capacities, local governments can raise long-term capital from the market for infrastructure projects that support local and regional sustainable development priorities. The benefits of developing debt capital markets for local government borrowing can include:

---

[7] W. Lam and J. Wang. 2018. China's Local Government Bond Market. *International Monetary Fund (IMF) Working Paper. No. 46275.* https://www.imf.org/en/Publications/WP/Issues/2018/09/28/China-s-Local-Government-Bond-Market-46275.

[8] Japan Ministry of Internal Affairs and Communications. 2019. *Local Government Bonds System in Japan.* https://www.chihousai.or.jp/english/07/pdf/2019_mic.pdf.

[9] O. Merk. et al. 2012. Financing Green Urban Infrastructure. *OECD Regional Development Working Papers. No. 2012/10.* https://doi org/10.1787/5k92p0c6j6r0-en.

[10] IMF. 2001. Chapter 11 Development of Subnational Bond Markets. In *Developing Government Bond Markets.* https://doi.org/10.5089/9780821349557.069.ch011.

[11] IMF and World Bank. 2021. Guidance Note for Developing Government Local Currency Bond Markets. *Analytical Notes 2021.* https://doi.org/10.5089/9781513573922.064.

- **lower financing** costs through diversification of funding sources, access to new sources of capital, and access to longer tenors (footnote 7);
- **strengthened governance** via on-balance-sheet issuance by local governments, which supports a culture of prudent debt use, accountability, transparency, and fiscal self-sufficiency, while reducing reliance on central government transfers (footnote 6);
- **capital market deepening** through the creation of local currency investment opportunities with greater liquidity for domestic asset owners, thus enabling differentiated credit pricing; and
- **greater civic engagement** through increased citizen involvement and awareness of projects, with the ability to invest in projects with direct environmental and social benefits for local communities.

Across local government bond markets, issuers are increasingly using GSS+ bonds to finance their sustainable development priorities. The GSS+ label is a versatile and widely accepted format that aligns with the specific sustainable financing needs of local issuers. It effectively connects public sector demand for long-term, competitively priced capital with private investor demand for high-quality, high-impact sustainable finance opportunities. In several major markets such as Australia, Japan, the Netherlands, and Sweden, GSS+ bonds now account for more than 10% of local government bond issuance every year (**Figure 2**).

Issuing GSS+ bonds further requires additional steps, however, as local governments need to develop sustainable financing frameworks, build impact data tracking and reporting capabilities, and identify a pipeline of eligible municipal investment projects with clear repayment sources.[12]

Figure 2: GSS+ Local Government Bond Issuance in Selected Markets, 2023–2024

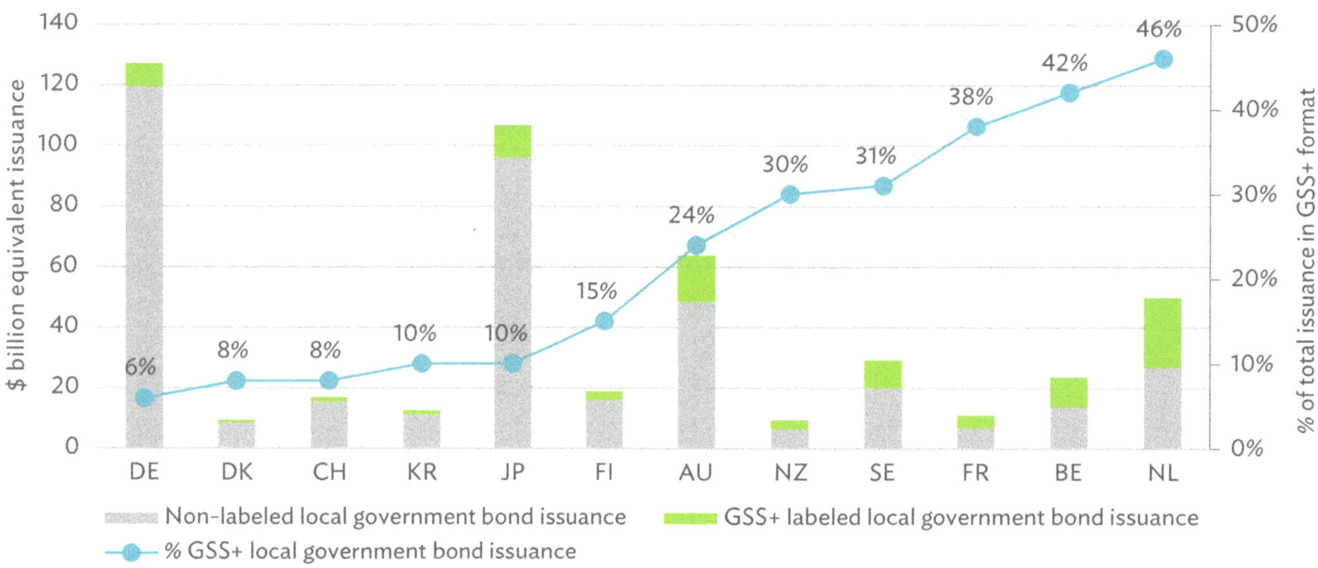

AU = Australia; BE = Belgium; CH = Switzerland; DE = Germany; DK = Denmark; FI = Finland; FR = France; GSS+ = green, social, sustainability, sustainability-linked, and other labeled bonds; JP = Japan; KR = Republic of Korea; NL = Netherlands; NZ = New Zealand.
Notes: Totals include bonds issued by municipal finance organizations. Data are as of 31 March 2025.
Source: Authors' calculations based on Bloomberg LP data.

[12] International Finance Corporation. 2018. Climate Investment Opportunities in Cities—An IFC Analysis. https://www.ifc.org/content/dam/ifc/doc/mgrt/201811-cioc-ifc-analysis.pdf.

L3: Cau Giay
km
15+300
KRIK

3. GLOBAL OVERVIEW OF LOCAL GOVERNMENT BOND MARKETS

Public borrowing is not limited to sovereign debt issuance by central governments. In many developed and emerging economies, sub-sovereign issuers such as cities, states, and regional authorities (or designated agencies) also issue local government bonds to finance infrastructure and municipal service delivery. This section presents a global overview of these local government bond markets, examines the role of municipal finance organizations, and analyzes the use of green, social, sustainability, sustainability-linked, and other labeled (GSS+) "use-of-proceeds" bonds for financing sustainable local infrastructure projects.

3.1 Mapping the Momentum: Global Trends in Local Government Bond Issuance

In terms of absolute size, the United States and the People's Republic of China dominate global annual issuance of local government bonds, reflecting the scale and depth of their domestic fixed-income markets. Local government bond issuance elsewhere is concentrated among a group of countries including Australia, Canada, Germany, India, Japan, and the Nordic countries (**Figure 3**). Issuance volumes in these markets have remained relatively stable since 2010, with a tendency to increase in response to acute economic, environmental, or social crises (**Figure 4**). Reflecting the predominantly domestic investor base in most markets, issuance of local government bonds is often denominated in the local currency.

Figure 3: Local Government Bonds Outstanding Globally (excluding the United States and the People's Republic of China)

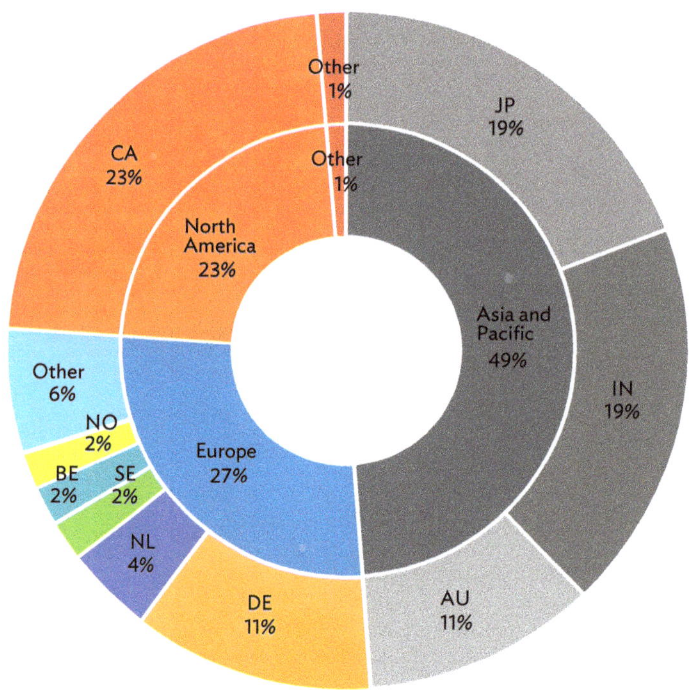

AU = Australia, BE = Belgium, CA = Canada, DE = Germany, IN = India, JP = Japan, NL = Netherlands, NO = Norway, SE = Sweden.
Note: Data are as of 31 March 2025.
Source: Authors' calculations based on Bloomberg LP data.

Figure 4: Annual Issuance of Local Government Bonds Globally (excluding the United States and the People's Republic of China)

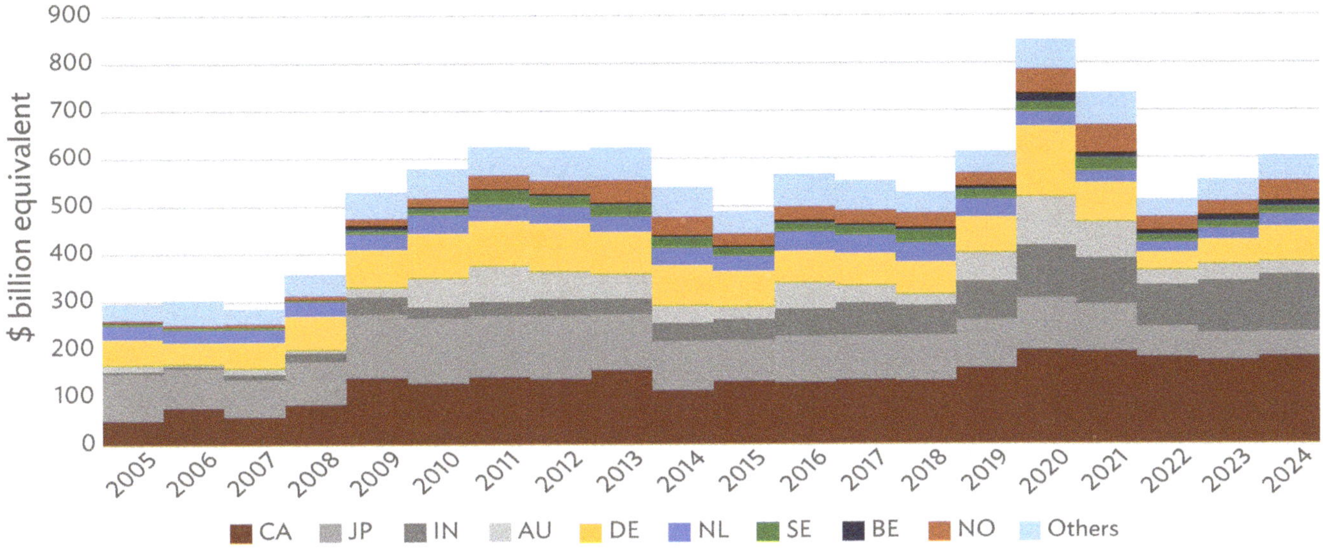

AU = Australia, BE = Belgium, CA = Canada, DE = Germany, IN = India, JP = Japan, NL = Netherlands, NO = Norway, SE = Sweden.
Notes: Data are as of 31 March 2025. Issuance amounts are based on United States dollar equivalent values at the time of issuance. Municipal bond market issuance tends to increase during times of crisis (e.g., global financial crisis, coronavirus disease [COVID-19] pandemic).
Source: Authors' calculations based on Bloomberg LP data.

3.2 Pooling Power: National Financing Vehicles for Local Governments

National pooled financing institutions are a well-established mechanism for enabling and scaling up local government access to long-term, diversified sources of capital. These collective financing vehicles are commonly used in the Japan and the Nordic countries, with several new examples established in recent years in other countries. Such institutions operate by aggregating the borrowing needs, credit profiles, and repayment obligations from member authorities in a single, well-capitalized municipal finance organization (**Table 1**). This structure enables the organization to issue bonds in domestic and international capital markets, then on-lend the proceeds to members with competitive rates and flexible terms. By consolidating demand and creditworthiness, these pooled vehicles enhance market access for smaller municipalities, reduce borrowing costs, and support the financing of sustainable infrastructure and service delivery across regions.

Establishing a municipal finance organization at the national level is a multifaceted process involving legislative, institutional, regulatory, and financial components, with central government bodies such as finance and interior ministries playing an important role. Through enabling legislation, they provide the policy foundation and legal basis for local governments to borrow jointly and establish dedicated entities for pooled local government financing or municipal bond agencies, as recently seen in France, New Zealand, and the United Kingdom.[13] Central governments also typically establish regulatory frameworks and

[13] Marten Andersson Productions. 2016. *Overview of Municipal Pooled Financing Practices*. https://www.maproductions.se/wpcontent/2016/04/Overview-of-municipal-pooled-financing-practices-study-tour-2015.pdf; New Zealand Local Government Funding Agency. About LGFA—Enabling Legislation. https://www.lgfa.co.nz/about-lgfa/enabling-legislation.

prudential borrowing guidelines for municipal financing organizations to ensure alignment with national public finance systems and policy priorities, and maintain oversight to ensure sound governance and robust risk management.

Table 1: List of Major Municipal Finance Organizations

Entity Name	Country	Year Established	Sustainable Finance Framework(s)	Total Debt Outstanding ($ billion)
Kuntarahoitus Oyj (MuniFin)	Finland	1989	Green, Social	55.0
KummuneKredit	Denmark	1898	Green	32.7
Agence France Locale (AFL)	France	2013	Sustainability	10.6
Kommuninvest	Sweden	1986	Green, Social	52.2
Japan Finance Organization for Municipalities (JFM)	Japan	1957	Green	126.7
Japan Major Joint Local Government Bond (JLGB)	Japan	2003	Green	82.9
New Zealand Local Government Funding Agency (LGFA)	New Zealand	2011	Sustainability, Sustainability-linked Loan	14.8
Kommunalbanken AS (KBN)	Norway	1927	Green	61.3
Nederlandse Waterschapsbank (NWB Bank)	Netherlands	1954	Green, Social	64.0
Bank Nederlandse Gemeenten (BNG Bank)	Netherlands	1914	Social, Sustainability	112.2
UK Minicpal Bond Agency	UK	2014	Green, Social	0.3
Municipal Finance Authority of British Columbia (MFA)	Canada	1970	Sustainability	7.0

UK = United Kingdom.
Notes: Data are as of 28 February 2025. All amounts have been converted to United States dollars.
Sources: Authors' calculations based on issuer websites and Bloomberg LP data.

Depending on the institutional structure, central government entities may directly contribute capital and extend explicit or implicit guarantees to municipal financing organizations. While financial involvement by the central government requires additional implementing legislation and can introduce moral hazard risks, it enhances the municipal finance organization's creditworthiness for improved market access and lower borrowing costs in the crucial initial stages of establishment.

Central government ministries often provide technical assistance and capacity building for newly established municipal financing organizations. They typically offer support programs for project assessment and preparation, systems development for risk management, financial reporting, and auditing. Moreover, they assist with training, procurement, and governance structures, especially during the launch phase of the organization.

In the context of developing economies, development finance institutions can provide multilayered support to governments seeking to establish their own municipal finance organizations or develop local government bond programs to mobilize long-term capital for urban infrastructure and services. Their assistance may include:

- **financial support**, including initial capital contributions, concessional loans, on-lending facilities, and partial credit guarantees to enhance the creditworthiness of municipal bond issuances;[14] and

- **technical assistance**, including help with project preparation, strategic urban development planning, and the development of taxonomy-aligned sustainable finance frameworks that match municipal investments with climate, adaptation, and resilience goals.

Another benefit of collective municipal financing vehicles is their ability to offer professional budgetary, financial, and sustainable finance-related advisory services for members with limited in-house capacities. This is being demonstrated in small and decentralized economies across Europe where several municipal finance organizations and public sector agency banks have become active issuers in foreign markets and currencies on behalf of their members. Following this strategy not only diversifies the investor base but also helps avoid oversaturation of domestic debt markets, thereby maintaining favorable borrowing conditions for local governments.

3.3 GSS+ Bonds for Local Government Infrastructure Investment Needs

GSS+ bonds are debt instruments that finance projects with environmental and social benefits. These instruments follow internationally recognized frameworks such as the Green and Social Bond Principles developed by the International Capital Market Association (ICMA), which define eligible green and social project categories for sustainable financing. Common project types include renewable energy, sustainable water infrastructure, green buildings, biodiversity conservation, clean transportation, and affordable housing.

Many of these project types have strong alignment with the infrastructure investment and service delivery of subnational governments, making GSS+ bonds a highly suitable vehicle for raising long-term capital for local development. And as awareness and demand for sustainable finance has grown, local government issuers have increasingly deployed the format for new financing, with GSS+ bonds now representing a significant share of annual issuance in many countries (**Figure 5**).

[14] A notable example is India's Tamil Nadu Urban Infrastructure Financial Services Limited, which benefited from such support mechanisms. Government of Tamil Nadu. 2024. *Pooled Municipal Bonds*. https://sdgknowledgehub.undp.org.in/wp-content/uploads/2024/11/8.-Tamil-Nadu-Pooled-financing-mechanisms-for-SDG-acceleration.pdf.

Figure 5: Cumulative Share of Local Government Bond Issuance in GSS+ Formats for Selected Markets

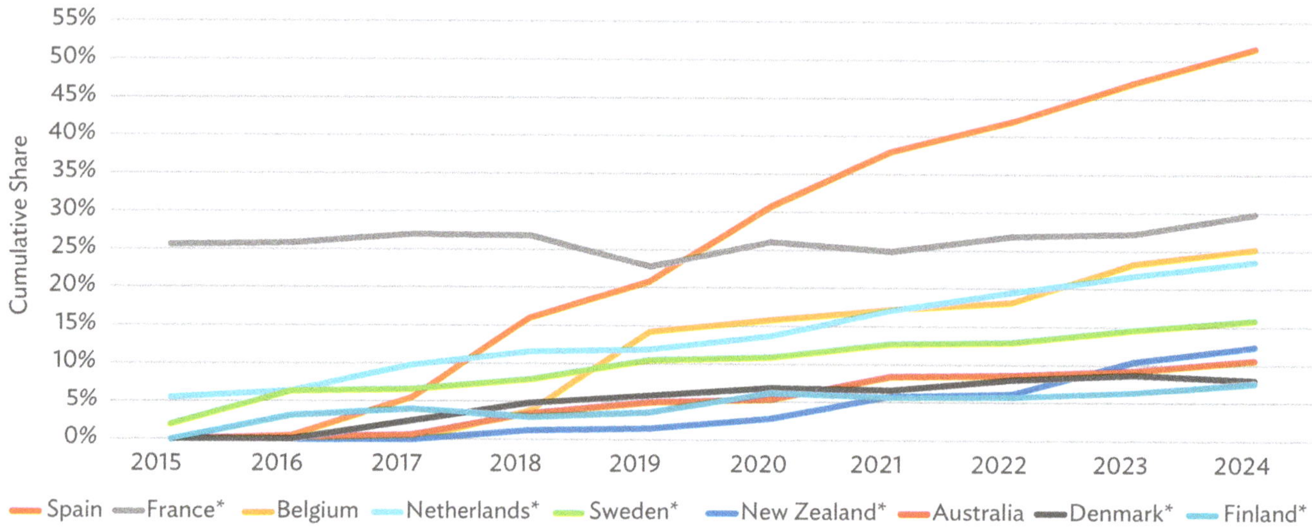

GSS+ = green, social, sustainability, sustainability-linked, and other labeled bonds.

* indicates markets where issuance by local municipal finance organizations is included.

Note: Data are as of 31 March 2025.

Source: Authors' calculations based on Bloomberg LP data.

As of the end of 2024, GSS+ instruments accounted for 6.7% of the global (excluding the People's Republic of China) outstanding stock of local government bonds and 6.9% of outstanding municipal bonds in the United States. This underscores the importance of labeled bonds to borrowers and investors alike for fostering climate-resilient, inclusive, and sustainable urban development in diverse country contexts (**Boxes 1 and 2**).

Box 1: Sustainable Financing in the United States Municipal Bond Market

The United States (US) municipal bond market is by far the largest, most developed, and diverse market for local government bonds in the world. As of 2024, it comprised approximately $4.2 trillion of outstanding bonds. About 80% of these bonds were issued by individual states, cities, and government-owned utilities to finance public infrastructure such as schools, power grids, water and sewage systems, roads, and ports. The remaining 20% were issued by private entities or nonprofit organizations for airports, hospitals, universities, and affordable housing developers, with the local government acting as a conduit under the Private Activity Bonds framework.[a]

A distinctive feature of the US municipal market is that approximately 85% of bonds pay interest income that is exempt from federal, and often state, income taxes for US-based investors. This tax advantage enhances the attractiveness of these bonds for domestic investors, generally supporting market demand and lowering borrowing costs for local government issuers. However, this makes municipal bond yields relatively less attractive to foreign investors, who are typically already tax-exempt and therefore lack an offsetting benefit to justify accepting structurally lower yields. As a result, foreign investors hold only around 2.5% of the US municipal bondmarket, leaving the investor base predominately domestic and retail-oriented.[b]

[a] SIFMA. US Municipal Bonds Statistics.

[b] Municipal Securities Rulemaking Board. 2022. Trends in Municipal Securities Ownership. Trends-in-Municipal-Securities-Ownership.pdf.

continued on next page

Box 1: continued

As US municipal bonds are often used to finance public and social infrastructure, the market includes a sizable share of GSS+ bonds, which comprise 6.9% of total outstanding issuance (4.0% green, 1.9% social, and 1.1% sustainability) (**Box Table**).

Analysis of the current outstanding stock of US municipal bonds shows that green labels are commonly used for public infrastructure and power, mass transit, water, and waste management projects, while social and sustainability labels are almost exclusively used in housing-related sectors. Interestingly, other large sectors of the market, including education and health care, do not typically issue under sustainable financing labels, despite their apparent linkages to social projects. This indicates that municipal bond issuers in the US do not simply rely on their status as "pure play" social institutions when choosing whether to label their issuance programs as sustainable finance.

Box Table: United States Municipal Bonds by Type of Label

US Municipal Bond Classification	Green	Social	Sustainability	Total
Housing (single, family, multi-family, student)	1%	21%	11%	33%
Energy (including clean energy projects)	24%	0%	0%	24%
Mass Transit	17%	1%	1%	18%
Water and Sewer	17%	0%	1%	17%
Project Infrastructure and Project Finance	14%	1%	0%	16%
Waste Management	12%	0%	0%	12%
Economic and Industrial Development	9%	0%	1%	9%
Airports	6%	0%	0%	6%
Electricity and Power Utility	6%	0%	0%	6%
Education	1%	1%	0%	3%
Health Care	1%	0%	0%	1%
Other (state, city, economy, local tax authority)	1%	1%	0%	1%
Labeled Municipal Bonds as a Percentage of Total Outstanding	4%	2%	1%	7%

Notes: The table shows the percentage of United States (US) municipal bonds that are labeled. For example, 4.0% of all outstanding US municipal bonds and 17.1% of mass-transit-related US municipal bonds have a "green" label. Data are as of 31 December 2024.
Source: Authors' calculations based on Bloomberg LP data.

Box 2: Huzhou Green Finance Pilot Zone—Sustainable Municipal Investment in the People's Republic of China

Since their introduction in 2017, the People's Republic of China's (PRC) green finance reform and innovation pilot zones have played a key role in stimulating finance at the local level for green investments and carbon reduction projects.

Huzhou, located in Zhejiang province, is one of the PRC's flagship green finance reform and innovation pilot zones. The city has developed its own comprehensive sustainable finance ecosystem at the local level—encompassing regulatory guidance and infrastructure, policy incentives, financial product innovation, and digital transformation and capacity-building initiatives—to accelerate the adoption of municipal green finance.

continued on next page

Box 2: continued

In addition to the national green taxonomy, Huzhou developed a local green finance policy framework and standards to evaluate green economic activities in 2017, followed by a local transition finance taxonomy in 2022.[c] This process involved referencing global best practices for green and transition finance, ensuring alignment with the local context, and developing the capacity of local stakeholders. Huzhou's localized decarbonization pathways and targets, alongside other regulatory guidance, are designed to be practical and transparent to improve confidence among the local financial sector and real-economy players when evaluating sustainable investments and financial incentives.

Facing a countrywide lack of climate adaptation projects and eligible adaptation investments, per the Ministry of Ecology and Environment, the local government in Huzhou developed an environmental, social, and governance evaluation model for assessing entities that identifies climate change adaptation as one of several key environment objectives, alongside sustainable resource use and pollutant emissions management.[d] It accompanied this with strengthened disclosure requirements for environmental risks and climate-related stress tests for financial institutions, encouraging the tagging of projects and investments that contribute to climate resilience.

As Huzhou's example shows, local sustainable debt market deepening requires continuous evolution and enhancement of institutional capacities. The city's success provides a model for other local governments in the PRC and the region to mobilize public finance through green, social, sustainability, and other labeled (GSS+) bonds and local initiatives.

Source: Authors' compilation.

[c] CFA Institute. Green and Transition Finance on the Municipal Level: Case of Huzhou City. https://rpc.cfainstitute.org/research/reports/2024/green-and-transition-finance-on-the-municipal-level.

[d] Dialogue Earth. *Climate Finance in China: How Are 23 Pilot Cities Doing?* https://dialogue.earth/en/climate/climate-finance-in-china-how-are-23-pilot-cities-doing/; Huzhou Green Finance Institute. Together for Green: Case Studies on Huzhou's Green Finance Reform and Innovation. https://en.hzgf.org.cn/storage/files/FGSC.pdf.

GSS+ bonds are a good fit for financing a wide range of subnational infrastructure development andupgrading projects, especially in sectors with direct relevance to local governments such as energy, water and sewerage infrastructure, transport, and social housing. Analysis of Climate Bonds Initiative (CBI)-certified regional and municipal government and utility bond issues shows that these sectors are strongly represented across issuers in all four of the case studies included in this report (**Table 2**).

Table 2: Use of Proceeds Commonly Referenced in GSS+ Local Government Bonds

Sector	Use-of-Proceeds Examples	Case Study Reference in This Report			
		Tokyo	Gothenburg	Cape Town	Île-de-France
Transport	Purchase of electric, hybrid, and other low-emissions vehicles for public transport and official use	X	X		X
	Provision of electric vehicle charging stations and other clean-transport-enabling infrastructure		X		
	Expansion and improvement of public transportation networks (rail, tram, bus, ferry, bicycle)	X			X

continued on next page

Table 2: continued

Sector	Use-of-Proceeds Examples	Case Study Reference in This Report			
		Tokyo	Gothenburg	Cape Town	Île-de-France
Energy	Development of new renewable energy generation capacity (solar, wind, hydro, geothermal)	X	X		X
	Development and promotion of electrical energy storage, transmission, and distribution capacity	X			
Water	Construction and rehabilitation of municipal water infrastructure			X	
	Improvement of sewerage infrastructure and wastewater treatment facilities			X	
	Development of flood control infrastructure and mitigation measures	X		X	
Buildings	Development of green buildings for public housing, schools, health facilities, and municipal buildings		X		X
Efficiency	Installation of LED lights in municipal facilities and transportation infrastructure	X	X		
	Installation of energy-efficient heating, cooling, and lighting in municipal buildings	X	X		
	Development of municipal district heating and cooling infrastructure		X		
Environment	Development of parks and green spaces, city tree planting, river and wetland cleanup and preservation	X	X		

GSS+ bonds = green, social, sustainability, sustainability-linked, and other labeled bonds.
Note: Categorization adopted from the International Capital Market Association's Green Bond Principles (June 2025 revision), based on a sample of 149 Climate Bonds Initiative-aligned local government bonds issued between 2016 and 2025.
Source: Authors' compilation.

3.4 GSS+ Bonds for Local Government Climate Adaptation and Resiliency

Despite progress in several areas, environmental action remains insufficient to meet global sustainability goals.[15] This implies that a significant increase in climate adaptation and resilience investment is necessary to respond to the destabilizing impacts of rising global temperatures. Yet, adaptation and resiliency projects are typically undertaken by the public sector and attract only a small fraction of overall financing flows. These projects face challenges in attracting private capital as they are often nonstandardized and dependent upon local context, and they typically create value as a common good indirectly through the reduction of climate risks and cost rather than through direct revenue generation. As a result, climate resilience budget tagging and taxonomy development to boost project pipelines is ongoing by the United Nations Office for Disaster Risk Reduction and the CBI.[16] A significant share of investments needed for climate adaptation and infrastructure resiliency will be delivered at the local level by municipal governments and other

[15] United Nations Climate Change. 2023. New Analysis of National Climate Plans: Insufficient Progress Made, COP28 Must Set Stage for Immediate Action. News release. 14 November. https://unfccc.int/news/new-analysis-of-national-climate-plansinsufficient-progress-made-cop28-must-set-stage-for-immediate.

[16] Climate Bonds Initiative. Climate Bonds Resilience Taxonomy. https://www.climatebonds.net/resilience; United Nations Officer for Disaster Risk Reduction. 2023. Global Taxonomies on Adaptation and Resilience Launched at COP28. 4 December. https://www.undrr.org/news/global-taxonomies-adaptation-and-resilience-launched-cop28.

subsovereign entities. GSS+ bonds can directly support local governments' climate adaptation priorities by financing projects such as sustainable water infrastructure, nature-based adaptation solutions, and disaster prevention measures (**Table 3**).

Table 3: Adaptation and Resilience Categories and Use of Proceeds for Local Government Bonds

Adaptation and Resilience Category	Damage Type	ICMA Use of Proceeds	CBI Resilience Taxonomy	Examples of Municipal Projects
Water Supply and Drought Resilience	Drought, Water Stress	Sustainable Water and Wastewater	Water Supply, Wastewater Collection and Treatment Infrastructure	Efficient and climate-resilient waterworks and sewerage, water reuse and recycling facilities, resilient water treatment distribution, leak reduction
Flood and Stormwater Management	Flood, Sea Level Rise	Climate Change Adaptation	Flood Management Infrastructure, Flood Resistant Systems	Levees, seawalls, and surge barriers; stormwater networks, permeable pavements, wetland and floodplain restoration; flood risk analysis
Heat Resilience and Urban Cooling	Heat Stress	Climate Change Adaptation	Urban Infrastructure, Buildings, Municipal Services	Expansion of parks and green corridors, urban tree canopy, cool roofs and pavements, climate shelters and cooling centers
Resilient Energy and Critical Infrastructure	Flood, Storm Damage	Climate Change Adaptation	Energy, Transport, and ICT Infrastructure, Buildings	Grid hardening, microgrids and backup for hospitals and emergency services, under-grounding powerlines and utilities, resilient transport and telecom nodes
Climate-Smart Buildings and Housing	Multiple	Climate Change Adaptation, Green Buildings	Municipal Facilities including Schools, Health, and Housing	Flood-proofing and elevating public housing and infrastructure; climate resilient schools and clinics; wind, flood, and heat-hardening retrofits to public buildings
Public Health and Early Warning	Multiple	Climate Change Adaptation, Social Co-Benefits	Public Admin. for Disaster Risk Reduction and Social Protections	Disaster preparedness measures, emergency supply stockpiling and distribution, emergency shelters, heatwave and air quality early-warning systems
Nature-Based Solutions and Ecosystem Protection	Multiple	Terrestrial and Aquatic Biodiversity	Freshwater, Marine, and Terrestrial Ecosystem Services	Mangrove, wetland, and dune restoration; nature-based wetland buffers and shoreline stabilization; expansion of urban biodiversity corridors and nature spaces

CBI = Climate Bonds Initiative, ICMA = International Capital Market Association, ICT = information and communication technology.
Note: Categorization adopted from the ICMA Green Bond Principles (June 2025 revision) and CBI Resilience Taxonomy Version 1.
Source: Authors' compilation.

Sub-sovereign issuers including local governments and public agencies account for 69% of global adaptation and resilience-related GSS+ bond issuance, compared with only 2% from sovereign and central government issuers. This underscores the GSS+ bond format's strong alignment with regional and municipal governments' adaption investment needs and its growing role in advancing climate-resilient development at the local level (**Figure 6**).[17]

[17] CBI. 2024. Climate Bonds Resilience Taxonomy Methodology. https://www.climatebonds.net/files/files/CBI_Res_Meth_24_03C%281%29.pdf.

Figure 6: Adaptation- and Resilience-Related GSS+ Bonds by Issuer Type

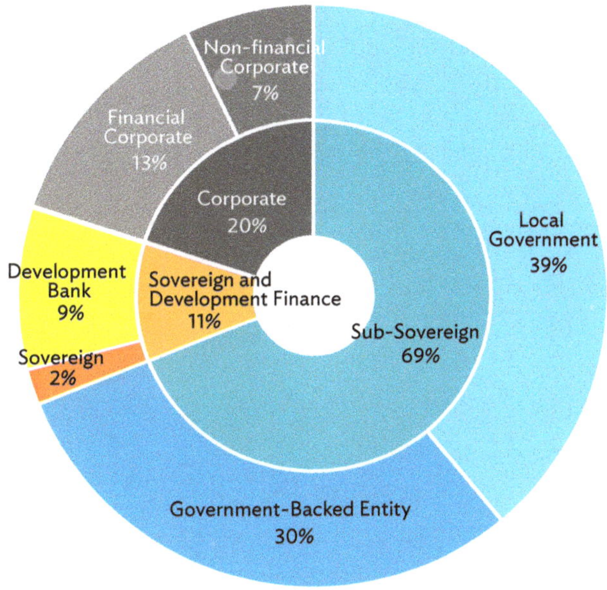

GSS+ bonds = green, social, sustainability, sustainability-linked, and other labeled bonds.
Source: Climate Bonds Initiative. Climate Bonds Resilience Taxonomy Methodology 2024. https://www.climatebonds.net/files/documents/supporting-documents/Climate-Bonds_Resilience-Methodology_2024.pdf.

Local governments can expand access to GSS+ and other financing instruments by developing sustainable finance frameworks that include adaptation and resilience use-of-proceeds categories that reflect local conditions while referencing international approaches such as the CBI's Resilience Taxonomy. Such frameworks can strengthen the pipeline of well-prepared, high-impact adaptation projects suitable for GSS+ bond financing and help accelerate financial flows to climate adaptation and disaster-resilient investments (**Box 3**).

Box 3: Japan's Local Government GSS+ Bond Market for Climate- and Disaster-Resilient Public Infrastructure

Japan is well known for being impacted by disasters such as earthquakes, volcanoes, typhoons, landslides, and tsunamis. In many cases, rising climate risks are magnifying these physical risks. In 2019, Super Typhoon Hagibis caused nearly 100 deaths and economic losses exceeding $15 billion resulting from flooding and river dike failures in Tokyo and central Japan due to 24-hour rainfall totals exceeding that of a 1,500-year storm, according to return-period estimates. A Japan Meteorological Research Institute report on the storm estimated that post-industrial global warming contributed to a 14% increase in the storm's precipitation.

When disasters triggered by natural and climate hazards strike, local governments are on the front lines for disaster risk and recovery. In response, a growing number of Japanese municipalities are turning to green, social, sustainability, sustainability-linked, and other labeled (GSS+) bonds to finance climate adaptation and mitigation infrastructure for disaster resilience and local decarbonization goals. In 2024, over 35 unique local government entities in Japan raised ¥663 billion ($4.4 billion equivalent) via GSS+ bonds, accounting for over 10% of Japan's total local government bond issuance for that year (**Box Figure1**).

continued on next page

Box 3: continued

Box Figure1: Issuance of GSS+ Local Government Bonds in Japan by Year and Issuer Type

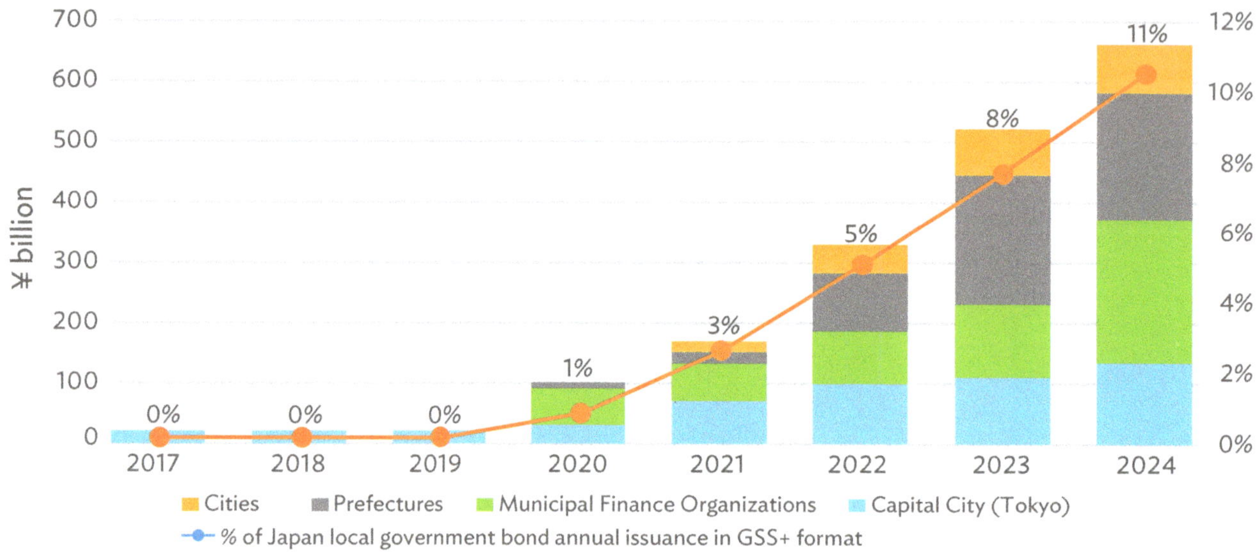

GSS+ = green, social, sustainability, sustainability-linked, and other labeled bonds.
Source: Authors' calculations based on Bloomberg LP data.

A unique aspect of the Japanese local GSS+ bond market is its relatively large allocation to climate adaptation projects. Analysis of green and sustainable financing frameworks from a sample of Japanese municipal GSS+ bond issuers shows that 70% of the use-of-proceeds categories for these bonds were allocated to projects for climate resiliency and adaptation, compared to 17% for climate change mitigation and 13% for mixed mitigation and adaptation projects. This significant focus on adaptation contrasts sharply with the emphasis on green bond allocation in the corporate bond market, where mitigation projects such as renewable energy, energy efficiency, and green buildings typically account for over 95% of all GSS+ allocation (**Box Figure2**).

Box Figure 2: Common GSS+ Use-of-Proceeds Categories for Local Government Bonds in Japan

Adaptation	Mitigation
River floodways and embankments	LED light installation in public buildings
Coastal storm surge prevention infrastructure	Solar and small hydro power plant installation
Forestry management and road rehabilitation	Purchase of new energy and energy-efficient vehicles
Erosion and anti-landslide measures	Green building construction and efficiency upgrades
Disaster-resilient roads and energy infrastructure	Parks and city greening improvements
Parks and heat island prevention	Sewer system upgrades for GHG and energy reduction
Kelp bed and local fisheries management	Energy-efficient air conditioning in public buildings

Environmental	
Adaptation	**Mitigation**
Environmentally Sustainable Management of Living Natural Resources	Land use Terrestrial and aquatic biodiversity

GHG = greenhouse gas; GSS+ bonds = green, social, sustainability, sustainability-linked, and other labeled bonds.
Source: Authors' calculations based on Bloomberg LP data.

This gap in adaptation financing points to a unique opportunity for local government GSS+ bonds to channel private capital to finance adaptation. Fundamentally, the long-term capital expenditure needs of local governments are well suited to deliver climate-resilient infrastructure such as inland and coastal flood defenses and measures to prevent erosion and landslides. Climate-resilient public infrastructure projects like these can directly contribute to the protection of life and property in local communities, with indirect financial and credit metric benefits from better disaster and recovery preparedness for the local government. They also represent a unique opportunity for fixed-income investors to fund high-impact climate adaptation and disaster resiliency at the local level.

4. LOCAL GOVERNMENT GSS+ BOND ISSUANCE CASE STUDIES

The following case studies illustrate how local government issuers around the world are tapping into the growing market for green, social, sustainability, sustainability-linked, and other labeled (GSS+) bonds to secure long-term, diversified financing and deliver local infrastructure investments for sustainable and resilient growth.

4.1 Case Study 1: Tokyo Metropolitan Government Green, Blue, Social, Sustainability, and Resilience Bonds

Table 4: Blueprint for Scaling Impact Bonds Nationwide

Tokyo Metropolitan Government (Japan) Green, Blue, Social, Sustainability, and Resiliency Bonds		
Pre-Issuance	Standards Alignment	ICMA Green (2021), Social (2023), Sustainability (2021) Bond Principles ICMA Practitioners Guide for Bonds to Finance the Sustainable Blue Economy (2024), Climate Bonds Resilience Criteria and Taxonomy (2025)
	External Review	Second-Party Opinion by ISS and R&I Green Bond Assessment by Moody's
Issuance (Recent)	Example ticker	TOKYO 2.625% 2030 Resilience #8 (5y)
	Currencies	Local: ¥ (Japanese yen); Foreign: $ (United States dollar), A$ (Australian dollar), € (euro)
	Details	TMG has consistently issued local-currency- and foreign-denominated GSS+ bonds every year since 2017
	Main Project Categories	Renewable Energy and Efficiency Sustainable Use of Resources and Biodiversity Infrastructure and Disaster Resilience
Post-Issuance	Allocation Reporting	Project allocations, context and impact goal completion rate, case studies
	Impact Reporting	Project-specific
	Independent Auditing	Post-issuance verification by ISS
	Accessible Disclosures	All relevant reports and supporting documents available online across multiple Tokyo Metropolitan Government websites

GHG = greenhouse gas; GSS+ bonds = green, social, sustainability, sustainability-linked, and other labeled bonds; ICMA = International Capital Market Association; ISS = Institutional Shareholder Services; TMG = Tokyo Metropolitan Government.

Source: Authors' compilation based on Tokyo Metropolitan Government. Green and Blue Bonds. https://www.english.metro.tokyo.lg.jp/w/006-101-000946.

4.1.1 Issuer Background

Metropolitan Tokyo is Japan's capital and largest city. It has a population exceeding 14 million, with GDP and GHG emissions rivaling those of many OECD countries. Tokyo prefecture is also geographically diverse, with densely populated urban cores, mountainous expanses, major ports and rivers, and remote islands stretching 1,000 kilometers into the Pacific Ocean.

Subnational responsibilities for economic-, social-, and climate-related expenditures are relatively extensive in Japan, and the Tokyo Metropolitan Government (TMG) intends to increase funding for policy initiatives to support child-raising and elder care, decarbonization, and infrastructure disaster resiliency.[18] TMG has a very high ratio of independent revenue sources (more than 90%). It receives credit ratings from international and domestic credit rating agencies, and it is an established local government bond issuer in the local currency and international debt markets.[19]

4.1.2 Local Challenges and Issuer Motivation

In addition to disaster risks from earthquakes, tsunamis, and volcanic eruptions. Tokyo, like many Asian cities, faces high and growing risks from climate-related physical risks due to storms, inland and coastal flooding, and urban heat-island effects. The city also faces socioeconomic and demographic challenges from Japan's "super-aging" population. However, TMG's status as the country's economic, administrative, and financial center affords it significant influence on the development of Japan's local government bond market as well as urban environmental policy and disaster resilience initiatives.

In 2007, TMG launched its Tokyo Climate Change strategy, which laid the foundation for Japan's first carbon cap-and-trade scheme.[20] This pioneering program targeted large-scale emitters and set mandatory GHG reduction targets, positioning Tokyo as a leader in urban climate policy. In 2016, TMG revised its Environmental Master Plan as a model for addressing a wider range of environmental initiatives at the local level.[21]

In 2019, TMG released two major policy documents: (i) the Zero Emissions Tokyo Strategy, which outlines a road map to achieve net-zero carbon emissions by 2050; and (ii) the Tokyo Climate Change Adaptation Policy.[22] These were followed by the Future Tokyo: Long Term Strategy in 2021 and the TOKYO Resilience Project in 2022 to further address social and environmental challenges as well as disaster resilience and safety through sustainable finance in a virtuous cycle with economic growth.[23] The city chose to issue GSS+ bonds to fund these policy initiatives and to catalyze growth in Japan's sustainable bond market (**Figure 7**).

---

[18] OECD. 2024. *OECD Regions and Cities at a Glance 2024*. https://doi.org/10.1787/f42db3bf-en; S&P Global Ratings. 2024. Tokyo Metropolitan Government. https://www.english.metro.tokyo.lg.jp/documents/d/english/sandp_20241031ee.

[19] TMG. 2024. *Tokyo Metropolitan Government*. https://www.zaimu.metro.tokyo.lg.jp/documents/d/english/ir_document2024_Dec_ver3.

[20] TMG Bureau of the Environment. 2007. Tokyo Formulates a Climate Change Strategy. News release. 1 June. https://www.kankyo.metro.tokyo.lg.jp/documents/d/kankyo/climate-climate_change-files-climatechangestrategypress

[21] TMG. 2022. *Tokyo Environmental Master Plan*. https://www.kankyo.metro.tokyo.lg.jp/documents/d/kankyo/masterplan-full_version.

[22] TMG. 2021. *Tokyo Climate Change Adaptation Plan*. https://www.kankyo.metro.tokyo.lg.jp/documents/d/kankyo/climate-100200a20220607180322567-files-tokyoclimatechangeadaptationplan.

[23] TMG Office of the Governor for Policy Planning. Basic Plan. https://www.seisakukikaku.metro.tokyo.lg.jp/english/basicplan;TMG Office of the Governor for Policy Planning. 2024. *Tokyo Resilience Project*. https://www.english.metro.tokyo.lg.jp/w/001-101-001118.

Figure 7: Tokyo Metropolitan Government GSS+ Bond Issuance by Year and Label Type

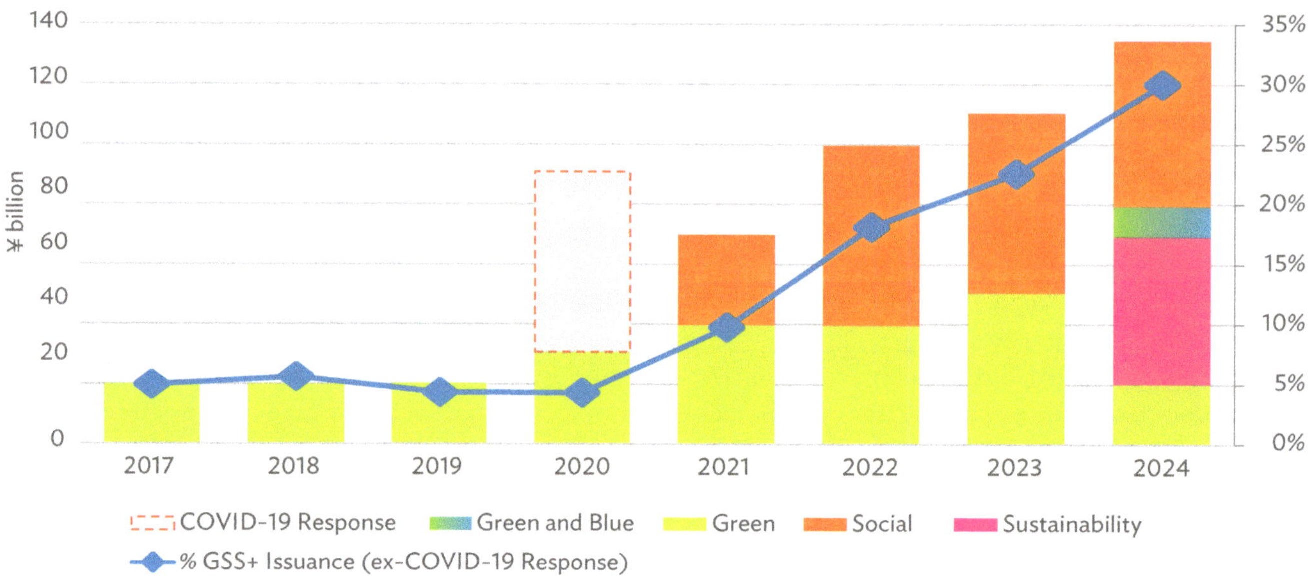

COVID-19 = coronavirus disease; GSS+ = green, social, sustainability, sustainability-linked, and other labeled bonds.
Source: Authors' calculations based on Bloomberg LP data.

4.1.3 GSS+ Financing Framework Development and Issuance Approach

TMG's labeled bond program has evolved into a highly comprehensive sustainable financing framework, reflecting the city's strategic priorities (**Table 5**). To finance the city's climate policy ambitions and respond to growing market demand for green assets, TMG developed its green bond framework in 2017, focusing on mitigation and adaptation projects that prioritize renewable energy and efficiency, environmental conservation, and climate resilience. The inaugural Tokyo Green Local Government Bond issued in 2017 was the first of its kind in Japan, with dual tranches of Japanese yen-dominated bonds for domestic retail investors and foreign currency bonds for international institutional investors, an issuance format that has been followed annually since then (**Figure 7**).

At the outbreak of the coronavirus disease (COVID-19) pandemic, TMG issued a COVID-19 Response Bond to provide emergency support for affected businesses. This was followed by the development of a social financing framework that was aligned with ICMA Social Bond Principles and reviewed by a second-party opinion provider to better target investors with environmental, social, and governance (ESG) mandates.[24]

In 2024, TMG developed a sustainability bond framework for financing environmental and social projects outlined in its Future Tokyo: Long Term Strategy.[25] The framework aligns with the ICMA's Green and Social Bond Principles as well as its Sustainability Bond Guidelines. The bond was issued in foreign currency, targeting international institutional investors. Most recently, the city has upgraded its green bond framework

[24] TMG. 2024. *Tokyo Social Bonds Framework*. https://www.zaimu.metro.tokyo.lg.jp/documents/d/zaimu/socialbondfw20240718; https://www.goldmansachs.com/insights/articles/from-briefings-05-august-2021.

[25] TMG. 2024. *Tokyo Sustainability Bonds Framework*. https://www.zaimu.metro.tokyo.lg.jp/documents/d/zaimu/sustainabilitybond_fw_202408_en-1-.

to include blue bonds for ocean ecosystem services, such as blue carbon projects, in line with the Practitioner's Guide for Bonds to Finance the Sustainable Blue Economy, and established a Tokyo Resilience Bonds Framework for climate and physical resilience projects.[26]

4.1.4 GSS+ Project Allocations and Impact Reporting

Green and sustainability bonds issued by TMG span a diverse portfolio of project types, with sustainable water management, renewable energy, and heat stress adaptation measures representing the top three categories by allocation amount in the 2024 impact reporting cycle (**Figure 8**). TMG's sustainable financing framework also assigns a relatively large weight to adaptation projects at 28% of the allocated total, reflecting the metropolitan government's focus on climate change and physical risks (**Figure 9**). In October 2025, TMG issued a seven times oversubscribed resilience bond in alignment with the CBI's Resilience Taxonomy and based on its existing sustainable finance framework to fund storm and flood disaster countermeasures.[27]

The city publishes annual impact reports in Japanese and English, which are available through its online investor relations portal, including detailed project case studies that report allocation and impact data, while also putting projects into the context of TMG's strategy and local goals for sustainability, adaptation, and resiliency.

Table 5: The Tokyo Metropolitan Government's Financing Framework

Eligible Categories	Primary Type	Sample Projects	Impact Indicators	SDG Alignment
Smart Energy and Urban Development	Mitigation	Rebuilding and repair of facilities (solar PV retrofit and installation), energy-saving water and sewage facilities	GHG emissions reductions (tCO_2e)	7, 13
	Mitigation	Installation of LED lights in facilities and roads	Energy consumption reduction and Energy generation (kWh)	7, 13
	Mitigation	Development and extension of cycling routes	Length of cycling routes (km)	7, 13
Natural Environment Conservation	Environment	Green space development, waterside greening, development of parks	Green space expansion (m2)	11
Improvement of the Living Environment	Adaptation	Heat island countermeasures	Developed and extended length of heat insulation and water absorption (km)	13
	Mitigation	Installation of environmentally friendly metropolitan buses	Reduction in regulated substance emissions (%)	12
	Adaptation	Improvement of centralized sewerage systems	Capacity of storage facilities (m3)	6
Adaptation for Climate Change	Adaptation	Counter measures against floods, development of rivers, tsunami protection facilities in ports and islands	Flood avoidance rate (%), Capacity of regulating reservoir (%), Number of facilities	13

km = kilometer, kWh = kilowatt-hour, m = meter, tC02e = tons of carbon dioxide equivalent.
Source: Authors' compilation.

26 Asian Development Bank. 2023. Bonds to Finance the Sustainable Blue Economy: A Practitioner's Guide. https://www.adb.org/publications/bonds-finance-sustainable-blue-economy-practitioners-guide.

27 R. Langston. 2025. Tokyo Metropolitan Government Plots €300m Resilience Bond. Environmental Finance. 19 June. https://www.environmental-finance.com/content/news/tokyo-metropolitan-government-plots-300m-resilience-bond.html.

Figure 8: Tokyo Metropolitan Government—Allocation by Green and Sustainability Bond Project Type

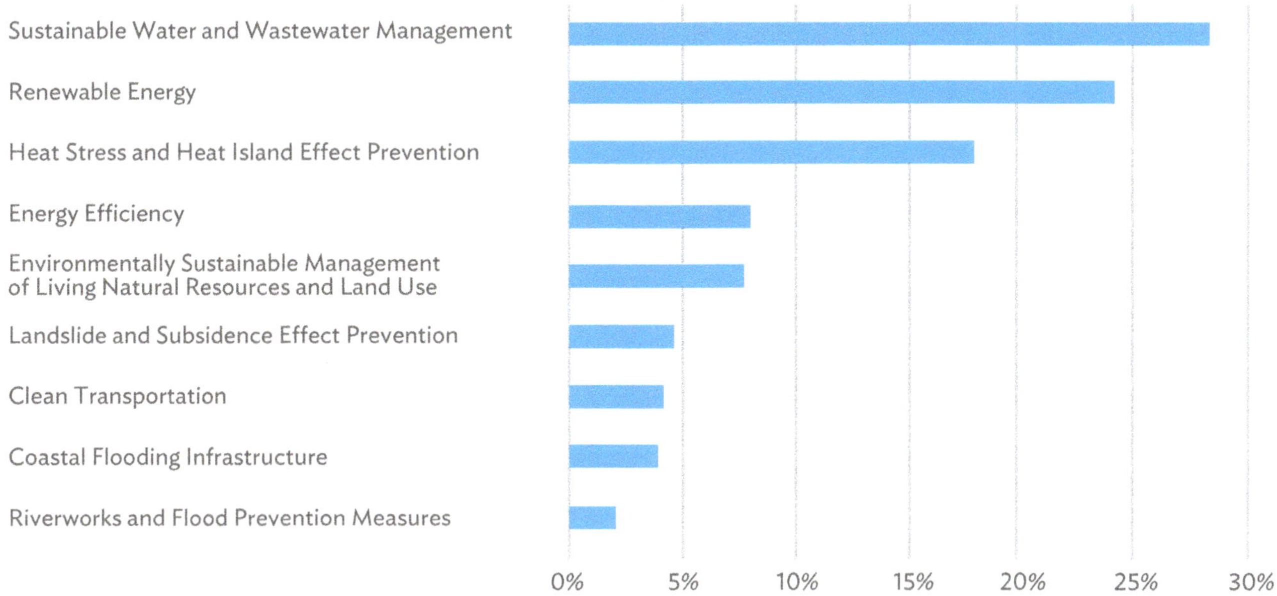

Source: Authors' calculations based on issuer sustainable financing framework and impact reports.

Figure 9: Tokyo Metropolitan Government—Allocation by Sustainable Finance Type (%)

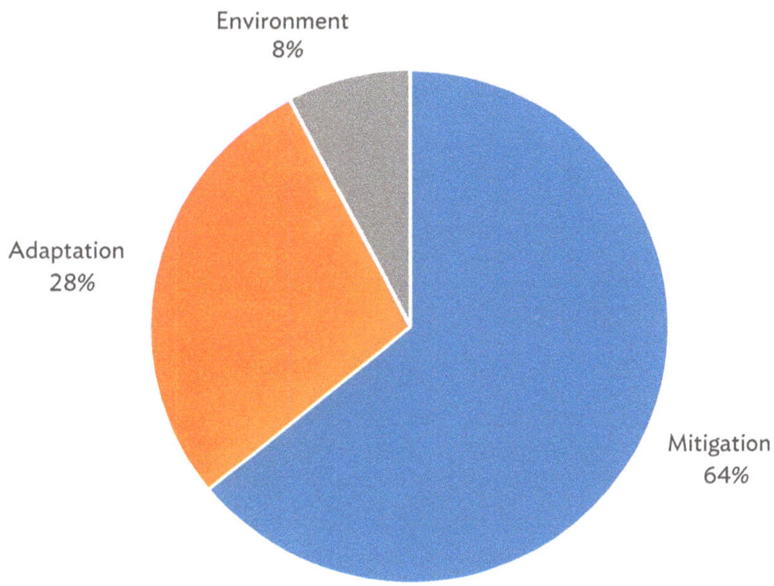

Source: Authors' calculations based on issuer sustainable financing framework and impact reports.

4.1.5 Assessment and Key Outcomes

TMG's latest green bond impact reporting for 2024 shows an overall allocation of 60% mitigation and 40% adaptation, with a split of 94% for green projects and 6% for blue projects. By project, the largest single allocation at 29% was for decarbonization projects including solar panel installations on metropolitan properties generating 5.2 million kilowatt-hours annually and ecosystem projects that increased green space by 10,442 square meters, with another 25% for river development and reservoir capacity.[28]

TMG's impact disclosures stand out not just for the level of detail provided but also for how the project's practical outcomes for improving city services are put into context and communicated to investors and citizens alike. As an additional outcome, TMG's pioneering issuance of green bonds has also had a catalytic effect in the domestic market, with over ¥1.8 trillion in domestic market GSS+ bond issuance from other local government issuers. However, local issuers like TMG sometimes face challenges gaining acceptance from international investors for certain types of adaptation and disaster resiliency projects, which are highly specific to local circumstances.

Figure 10: Tokyo Metropolitan Government Green Bond Issuance as a Catalyst for Local Government Issuance in Japan

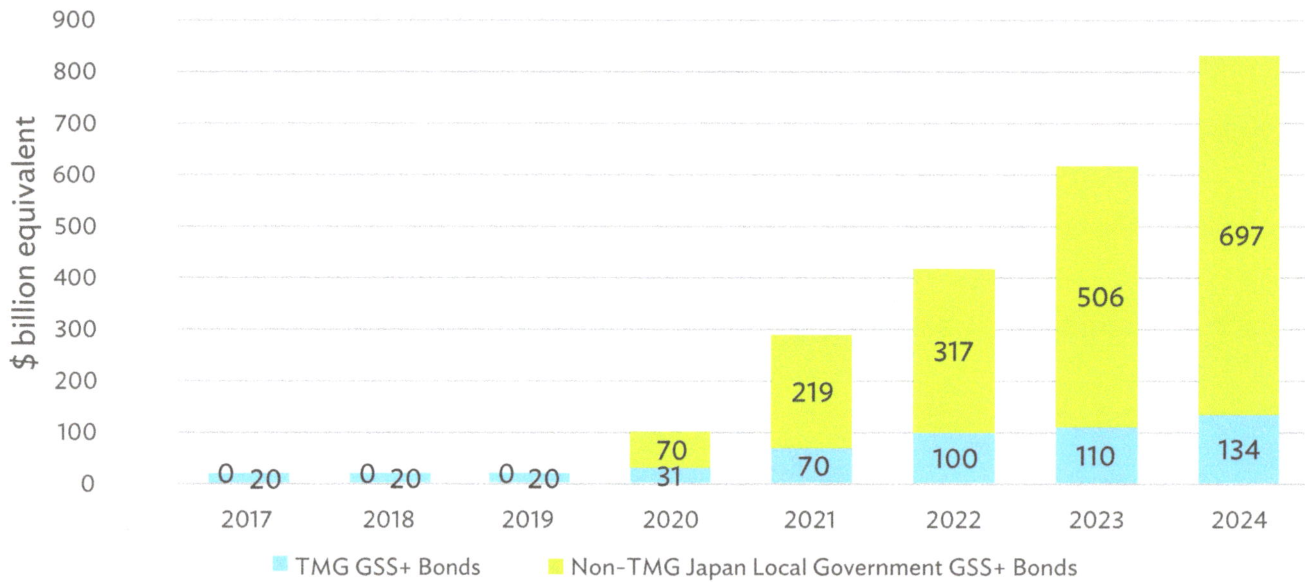

GSS+ = green, social, sustainability, sustainability-linked, and other labeled bonds; TMG = Tokyo Metropolitan Government.
Source: Authors' calculations based on Bloomberg LP data.

4.1.6 Lessons Learned

Large cities can catalyze domestic GSS+ markets. TMG has played a strategic role in catalyzing GSS+ bond markets. By pioneering local government issuance and consistently engaging both domestic and international investors, TMG has helped increase the volume of GSS+ bonds issued by other municipalities (**Figure 10**). This leadership has also contributed to expanding the domestic investor base and enhancing market familiarity with sustainable debt instruments.

Focus on ICMA/CBI-standard GSS+ bonds for global compatibility. TMG has an established presence among foreign investors, in addition to its local investor base. This approach ensures compatibility with global ESG investment mandates and avoids market fragmentation that can result from bespoke or nonstandard thematic bonds. Standardization has helped Tokyo position itself as a credible and transparent issuer in international sustainable finance markets.

[28] TMG. 2024. Tokyo Green Bond Impact Report. https://www.zaimu.metro.tokyo.lg.jp/documents/d/zaimu/impactreport_green_2024.

Emphasize the synergy between sustainability and economic growth. TMG aims to create a virtuous cycle where environmental stewardship supports economic resilience and growth by integrating this approach into an urban planning strategy based on the belief that environmental and social investments can drive economic development. This framing helps build broader support for sustainable finance and encourages participation from local investors and stakeholders.

4.2 Case Study 2. Gothenburg (Sweden) Green Bond

Table 6: Where It All Began—The World's First Local Government Green Bond

City of Gothenburg (Sweden) Green Bonds		
Pre-Issuance	Standards Alignment	ICMA Green Bond Principles (2021)
	External Review	Second-Party Opinion by CICERO
Issuance (Recent)	Example ticker	GOTA 2.858% 2030 (6y)
	Currencies	Swedish krona
	Details	Over 80% of the City of Gothenburg's outstanding bonds were green-labeled at year-end 2024.
	Main Project Category	Green and energy efficient buildings (80%)
Post-Issuance	Allocation Reporting	Project allocations, issuer's sustainability strategy, new project case studies
	Impact Reporting	Portfolio-aggregate and project-specific
	Independent Auditing	Limited assurance audit by PWC and Ernst & Young
	Accessible Disclosures	All relevant reports and supporting documents are available online across multiple Gothenburg investor relations websites.

ICMA = International Capital Market Association.
Source: Authors' compilation based on City of Gothenburg–Investor Relations Portal. https://goteborg.se/wps/portal/enhetssida/investor-relations/green-bonds.

4.2.1 Issuer Background

Gothenburg, the second-largest city in Sweden with a population of over 600,000, is an industrial and port city located in the west of the country, between the neighboring capitals of Oslo (Norway) and Copenhagen (Denmark). As a major Scandinavian port, its economy has traditionally relied on manufacturing and trade. In Sweden, municipalities like Gothenburg are mandated by the central government to deliver a comprehensive set of social services and public infrastructure. They are subject to balanced budget requirements, but municipalities are also granted a high degree of taxation autonomy and tax equalization.[29]

To finance sustainable infrastructure and urban development projects, Gothenburg can access institutional borrowing through Kommuninvest, Sweden's municipal finance agency, and other regional multilateral development banks.[30] In addition to these sources, Gothenburg also maintains a capital market program for issuing its own local government bonds. This dual approach provides flexibility and diversification in funding sources and has positioned Gothenburg as one of the largest municipal issuers in the Nordic region.[31]

[29] Stockholm Environment Institute. 2021. Municipal Finance in Sweden Fact Sheet. https://www.sei.org/wp-content/uploads/2021/05/factsheet-municipal-finance.pdf.

[30] City of Gothenburg. Investor Relations—Funding. https://goteborg.se/wps/portal/enhetssida/investor-relations/funding.

[31] City of Gothenburg. Investor Relations—Funding—Sources of Funding. https://goteborg.se/wps/portal/enhetssida/investorrelations/funding/sources-of-funding.

4.2.2 Local Challenges and Issuer Motivation

With Sweden's fastest-growing population, the City of Gothenburg faces increasing demands for housing and social infrastructure. As a major city in Northern Europe, it faces physical climate risks from increased storm activity and flooding, necessitating investment in climate resilience in urban planning. Furthermore, strong political support in Sweden for strict environmental standards, such as GHG reduction and pollution control, presents transition risks to Gothenburg's economy given its reliance on heavily emitting industries.

Motivated by these challenges, Gothenburg became a global pioneer in sustainable municipal finance by issuing the world's first municipal green bond in 2013 for funding the city's climate and environmental goals. Building on this leadership, Gothenburg also launched the Nordic region's first sustainability-linked loan in 2022, further reinforcing its commitment to aligning financial instruments with long-term sustainability outcomes.

4.2.3 GSS+ Financing Framework Development and Issuance Approach

Gothenburg's green financing framework is designed to support the city's climate objectives of reaching netzero emissions by 2030 through reductions in the energy intensity of buildings, a shift to 100% renewable energy, and reduced GHG emissions from transportation through modal shifts and decarbonization (**Table 7**).[32] The city has expanded its green bond portfolio, issuing larger volumes each year to reach a cumulative total of SKr24.95 billion ($2.4 billion equivalent) in 2023, representing 69% of its total bond volume.

Although Gothenburg's green bonds are exclusively denominated in local currency and issued in relatively modest sizes, typically ranging from SKr250 million to SKr1.8 billion, they attract strong interest from both domestic and international institutional investors and are held in several prominent global green bond funds, underscoring Gothenburg's credibility and leadership in sustainable municipal finance.

Table 7: City of Gothenburg's Financing Framework

City of Gothenburg (Sweden) Financing Framework				
Eligible Categories	**Primary Type**	**Sample Projects**	**Reported Impact (tCO_2e/ SKr million)**	**SDG Alignment**
Green and Energy Efficient Buildings	Mitigation	Energy -efficient and green housing projects, schools, municipal buildings, and real estate development	0.07	7, 11, 12, 13
Clean Transportation	Mitigation	Pedestrian bike lanes, electric cars for city carpools, electric car charging stations	0.72	9, 11, 13
Water and Wastewater Management	Adaptation	Sewer pump station, wastewater infrastructure, water pipe renewal	...	6, 14
Renewable Energy	Mitigation	Solar energy parks, rooftop solar installation, energy efficient and renewable energy boilers, co-generation plant	23.7	7, 13

continued on next page

[32] City of Gothenburg. Investor Relations—Green Bonds—Second Opinion. https://goteborg.se/wps/portal/enhetssida/investorrelations/green-bonds/second-opinion.

Table 7: continued

City of Gothenburg (Sweden) Financing Framework				
Eligible Categories	**Primary Type**	**Sample Projects**	**Reported Impact (tCO_2e/ SKr million)**	**SDG Alignment**
Energy Efficiency	Mitigation	District heating and cooling infrastructure, LED traffic lights	0.094	7, 9, 11, 13
Sustainable Land Use and Environmental Management	Environment	Wetland cleanup and reclamation, city tree planting	...	11, 14, 15

... = not available, tCO_2e, m^2 = square meter, m^3 = cubic meter, SDG = Sustainable Development Goal, SKr = Swedish krona.
Source: Authors' compilation.

Figure 11: City of Gothenburg—Green Bond Project Allocations

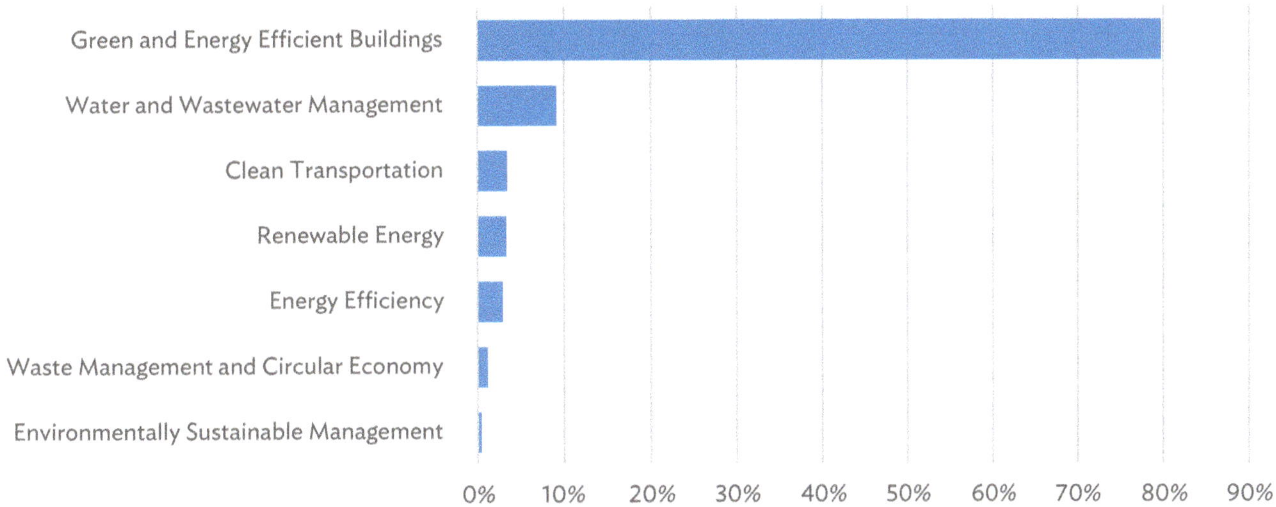

Source: Authors' calculations based on issuer sustainable financing framework and impact reports.

Figure 12: Gothenburg—Allocation by Sustainable Finance Type (%)

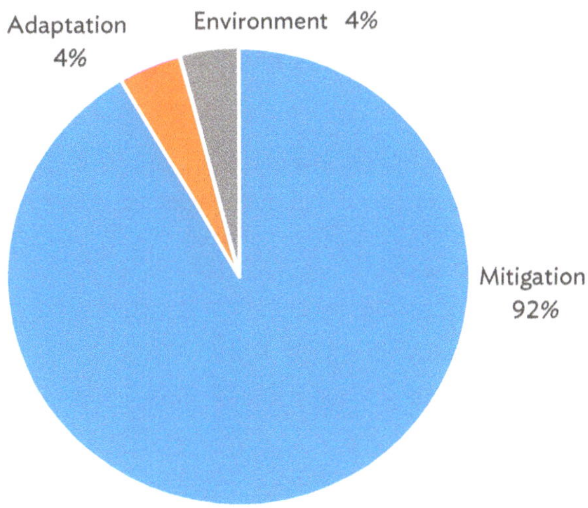

Source: Authors' calculations based on issuer sustainable financing framework and impact reports.

4.2.4 GSS+ Project Allocations and Impact Reporting

Green bond allocations by the City of Gothenburg are primarily directed toward energy-efficient buildings, which account for 79.6% of the portfolio, followed by water and wastewater management at 10%, with the remainder for renewable energy, energy efficiency, and clean transportation projects (**Figure 11**). The city provides comprehensive and unified impact reporting data that are updated annually in both Swedish and English via its investor relations website. Notably, the issuer disclosures include a breakdown of portfolio allocation by project type, new project highlights, emissions factors used, and individual project details, and aggregates impact indicators in absolute and intensity per SKr million for consistent comparison.

4.2.5 Assessment and Key Outcomes

The portfolio's strong emphasis on climate mitigation through energy efficiency in the built environment, accounting for nearly 80% of allocations, is contextually appropriate, given the country's already highly decarbonized energy systems and its considerable demand for indoor heating and lighting during the Arctic winter (**Figure 12**).

This focused approach on Gothenburg's most material and potential high-impact project categories demonstrates sophistication and thoughtfulness in addressing the issuer's key sustainable challenges. However, observers have raised concerns about the concentration of funding in green buildings for public housing, which has a high share of refinancing and has led to higher rent costs that affect housing affordability for disadvantaged populations.[33] Furthermore, the limited allocation to climate adaptation is seen as a missed opportunity, as these disaster resilience projects are typically only carried out by the public sector and lack alternative sources of financing. In contrast, green building investments often attract private capital, suggesting that public green bond funding could be more strategically directed toward underserved adaptation needs.

4.2.6 Key Lessons Learned

Clear and practical disclosure builds trust. Gothenburg's green bond impact reporting is a model of high standards for transparency in sustainable finance, benefiting both investors and local citizens. For example, the city's Green Bond Impact 2023 report includes a feature on investment in a new biofuel-fired steam boiler, including project disbursement amounts and timelines, along with how the project will contribute to achieving Gothenburg's climate policy goals for renewable energy use.[34] In markets with a strong preference for sustainability, such as Sweden, the quality and usability of sustainability disclosures are crucial for attracting investors and avoiding greenwashing.

Consistent issuance demonstrates commitment to sustainable finance. Gothenburg was the first local government issuer of green bonds and has shown a strong commitment to the green format, which now represents over 80% of the city's outstanding bonds, contributing to the mainstreaming of green finance in Sweden. Consistent GSS+ issuance can also help to develop the issuer's green credentials and strengthen engagements with stakeholders, including investors and local citizens.

---

33 Interlace. Urban Governance Atlas—Green Bond Framework—Gothenburg. https://interlace-hub.com/green-bond-frameworkgothenburg.

34 City of Gothenburg. 2023. Green Bond Impact Report 2023.

Consider the social dimensions of green buildings for housing. A significant majority of Gothenburg's green bond proceeds are allocated to green buildings, including investment in new and existing public housing. While these investments support climate goals, they have also been associated with increased rental costs for some single-parent and low-income households.[35] Issuers are encouraged to evaluate potential indirect impacts of sustainability programs—such as affordability—to ensure inclusive outcomes and maintain broad public support.

4.3 Case Study 3. Cape Town (South Africa) Green Bond

Table 8: Responding to Drought with Green-Funded Water Infrastructure

City of Cape Town (South Africa) Green Bonds		
Pre-Issuance	Standards Alignment	CBI Climate Bonds Standard v2.1
	External Reviews	Certification by CBI Green Bond Assessment by Moody's
Issuance (Recent)	Ticker	CAPTWN 10.17% 2027 (10y)
	Currencies	Local: R (South African rand)
	Details	Inaugural Green Bond was 4x oversubscribed and priced at R186+133 basis points (7 basis points inside initial guidance)
	Main Project Category	Water Infrastructure and Water Savings (85%)
	Allocation Reporting	Project names, some details, and ongoing allocation amounts
	Impact Reporting	Eligible projects and assets, and general impact indicators
	Independent Auditing	Limited assurance audit by KPMG
	Accessible Disclosures	All relevant reports and supporting documents available online are consolidated on the City of Cape Town investor relations website

CBI = Climate Bonds Initiative.

Source: Authors' compilation based on City of Cape Town. Work and Business—Invest in Cape Town. capetown.gov.za/Work and business/Investin-Cape-Town/The-Citys-investor-relations/External-finance.

4.3.1 Issuer Background

Cape Town, a port city of about 4.7 million people on the southwest coast of South Africa, is the country's second-largest city and a major economic hub with a diversified service-based economy driven by finance, manufacturing, trade, and tourism. Per capita income levels and 10-year economic growth rates exceed national averages, supported by relatively strong governance, reliable infrastructure, and the city's iconic natural setting.[36] These factors have contributed to Cape Town's sustained population growth, including significant internal migration from other regions of South Africa.

The city finances spending with a mix of local tax revenues, transfer grants, and debt, primarily for long-term infrastructure projects in the energy and water sectors.[37] Although South Africa has a highly developed local currency bond market, particularly for sovereign and corporate issuances, the market remains heavily

[35] M. García-Lamarca and S. Ullström. 2022. Everyone Wants This Market to Grow: The Affective Post-Politics of Municipal Green Bonds. Environment and Planning: Nature and Space. 5 (1). pp. 207–224. https://doi.org/10.1177/2514848620973708.

[36] Government of South Africa. 2023. Economic Performance Indicators for Cape Town 2023 Quarter 2 (April–June). https://www.capetown.gov.za/work%20and%20business/doing-business-in-the-city/business-support-and-guidance/economic-reports.

[37] Moody's Ratings. 2024. Credit Opinion (Sub-Sovereign): City of Cape Town (South Africa), July 2024. https://resource.capetown.gov.za/documentcentre/Documents/Financial%20documents/Schedule_1%20Moodys_Final_Credit_Opinion.pdf.

dominated by central government bonds. Bonds issued by local authorities, such as the city of Cape Town, represent less than 1% of the total market.[38] This limited participation underscores the untapped potential for subnational entities to leverage capital markets for sustainable infrastructure and development finance.

4.3.2 Local Challenges and Issuer Motivation

Cape Town faces high levels of first-order climate physical risk from drought, fire, heat waves, floods, and sea level rise, which is exacerbated by the city's population growth, local economic structure, and endemic socioeconomic inequalities in South Africa. Besides a concentration of future physical climate risks to communities in Cape Town's lower-income municipal periphery, water shortages pose an immediate threat to both the city's ability to provide municipal services and raise revenues.[39] Between 2015 and 2017, the city experienced a once-in-400-years drought, leading to emergency water rationing under the threat of almost total collapse of the municipal water supply.[40] In response, the city of Cape Town issued a green bond in 2017 to raise R1.0 billion ($77.1 million equivalent) for water meter improvements, water supply networks, and water conservation efforts.

4.3.3 GSS+ Financing Framework Development and Issuance Approach

Cape Town's green financing framework addresses the city's specific climate mitigation and adaptation challenges and C40 sustainable city commitments with long-term funding for water and sanitation infrastructure and updates (**Table 9**).[41]

During the design phase of the framework, it was determined that, along with water conservation awareness campaigns, preventative investments in water pressure management and leak detection systems were among the most cost-effective strategies for extending asset life and reducing water losses in municipal water systems.[42] Based on this analysis, the city prioritized allocations for such projects, recognizing their major impact and long-term value in improving system efficiency and resilience. Overall, the framework aligns with the city's long-term planning documents, including the Integrated Metropolitan Environmental Policy, 2001; Climate Change Policy, 2017; and Resilience Strategy, 2019.[43]

Prior to issuance, the framework obtained accreditation from the CBI for compliance with the Green Bond Standards' core use of proceeds and was externally reviewed at the highest "GB 1" green bond rating from Moody's, signaling strong alignment with international practices. After holding local investor roadshows, the city of Cape Town issued a 10-year, rand-denominated bond, which was four times oversubscribed, attracting a diverse mix of local banks, asset owners, and pension funds.[44]

38 Bloomberg LP.

39 AFD. 2019. City of Cape Town: Climate Change Hazard, Vulnerability and Risk Assessment. https://resource.capetown.gov.za/documentcentre/Documents/Procedures,%20guidelines%20and%20regulations/ClimateChangeHazardVulnerabilityRiskAssessment-ClimateResilienceInvestmentManual.pdf.

40 G. Hill-Lewis. 2023. Cape Town Lessons from Managing Water Scarcity. Brookings Institution Commentary. https://www.brookings.edu/articles/cape-town-lessons-from-managing-water-scarcity/.

41 City of Cape Town. 2017. City of Cape Town: Applicable Pricing Supplement Execution #4387209v1. https://resource.capetown.gov.za/documentcentre/Documents/Financial%20documents/CCT04%20Bond%20-%20Pricing%20Supplement.pdf.

42 N. Samir et al. 2017. Pressure Control for Minimizing Leakage in Water Distribution Systems. Alexandria Engineering Journal. 56(4). pp. 601–612. https://doi.org/10.1016/j.aej.2017.07.008.

43 City of Cape Town. 2017. City of Cape Town Climate Change Action Plan. https://resource.capetown.gov.za/documentcentre/Documents/City%20strategies,%20plans%20and%20frameworks/CCT_Climate_Change_Action_Plan.pdf.

44 United Nations Office for Disaster Risk Reduction. 2020. City of Cape Town Green Bond Issuance. https://www.undrr.org/media/48285/download?startDownload=20250217; Global Banking Markets. 2025. Case Study: Cape Town. https://globalbankingmarkets.com/news/case-study-cape-town-wins-race-to-issue-africas-first-municipal-green-bond.

Table 9: City of Cape Town Financing Framework

City of Cape Town (South Africa) Financing Framework				
Eligible Categories	**Primary Type**	**Sample Projects**	**Reported Impact**	**SDG Alignment**
Water Distribution	Adaptation	Pressure Management: Zone Metering and Valves	...	6, 11, 13
Water Capture and Storage	Adaptation	Upgrade of Reservoirs, Effluent treatment infra-structure	...	6, 9, 11
Water Treatment Plants	Mitigation	Replacement and upgrades to Sewer and Water Supply Network	...	6, 9, 11, 13
Flood Defenses	Adaptation	River Upgrade Projects	...	13

... = not available, SDG = Sustainable Development Goal.
Source: Authors' compilation.

Figure 13: Cape Town—Green Bond Project Allocations

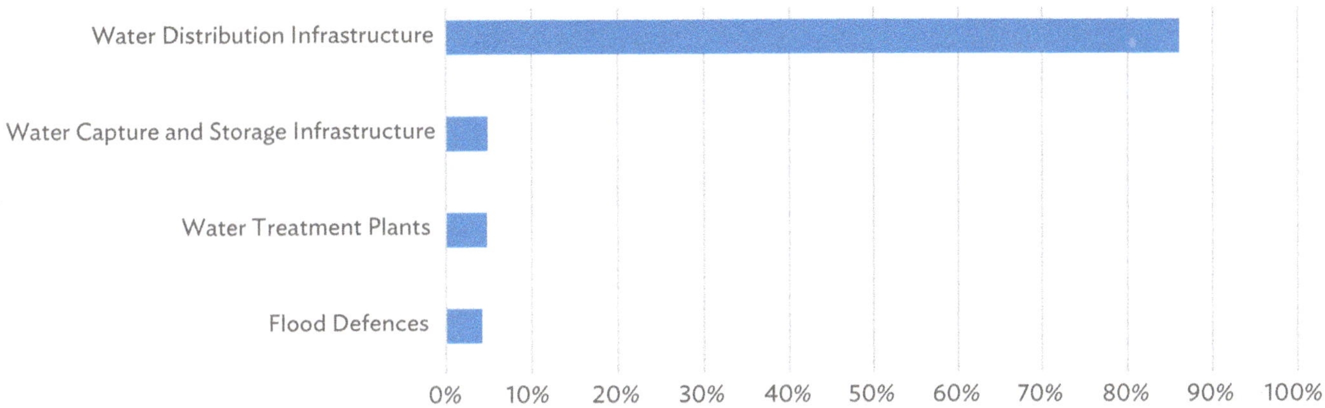

Source: Authors' calculations based on issuer sustainable financing framework and impact reports.

Figure 14: Cape Town—Allocation by Sustainable Finance Type

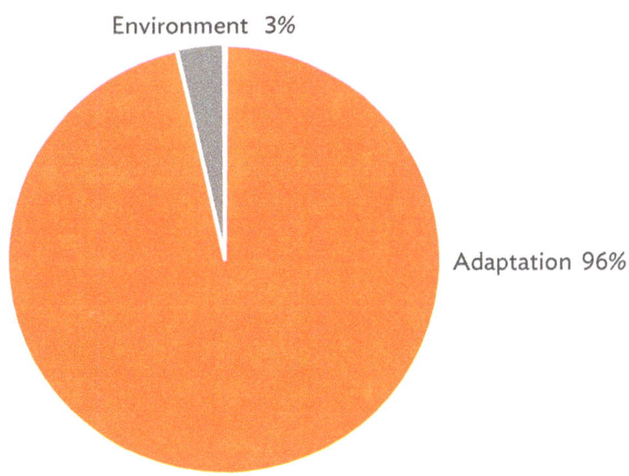

Source: Authors' calculations based on issuer sustainable financing framework and impact reports.

4.3.4 GSS+ Project Allocations and Impact Reporting

Cape Town's green bond is entirely dedicated to financing water-related infrastructure and water management projects. Of the total proceeds, 85% is allocated to water distribution infrastructure, primarily water meter replacement and conservation programs, with the remaining 15% for water treatment plants, reservoir upgrades, and flood defenses, based on annual project disbursement disclosures (**Figure 13**). Within 5 years of the green bond being issued, the city had established 170 pressure management zones covering 68% of the city's water system in 2021, although specific quantitative impacts attributable to the bond's projects have yet to be reported (Footnote 44).

4.3.5 Assessment and Key Outcomes

Cape Town's green bond portfolio, which is focused on water-related adaptation infrastructure, reflects the city's strategic focus on addressing this particular physical risk, with direct implications for sustainable growth, disaster resilience, and municipal revenue stability—a factor highly valued by investors (**Figure 14**).

The city government reported that the development of the green bond framework led to improvements in governance and transparency through enhanced project tracking and data sharing among internal departments, and raised public awareness of sustainability, facilitating the launch of Cape Town's Climate Change Policy. In 2018, the bond program was awarded Green Bond of the Year–Local Authority by Environmental Finance, and since 2019 Cape Town has been listed as the only city in Africa to be A-rated by the Carbon Disclosure Project for climate action and data transparency.[45] The benefits from such recognition can boost market confidence in an issuer's climate strategy and investability, with potential benefits to investor base diversification and access to finance that extend beyond the cost of an individual bond deal.

4.3.6 Key Lessons Learned

Be prepared to turn crisis into opportunity with GSS+ bonds. Sustainable financing is often an effective way to quickly mobilize capital, as seen with the rapid rise of social bonds to finance pandemic-era spending and recovery efforts. Similarly, the city of Cape Town's green bond for countering a local water crisis demonstrates how green bonds can be used to address environmental crises. Establishing sustainable financing frameworks and GSS+ bond issuance programs in advance can assist issuers seeking to rapidly raise funds in times of acute crisis.

Leverage the nonfinancial benefits of GSS+ issuance. Besides achieving tighter pricing and a more diversified investor base, GSS+ bonds also offer valuable nonfinancial benefits. Cape Town's green bond helped raise public awareness of the city's climate strategy and water conservation campaign and initiated the "greening" of the Treasury department to develop more sustainable projects for GSS+ bond financing in the future. Recognizing the full set of potential benefits, both financial and nonfinancial, can bolster the case for local treasuries considering whether to issue GSS+ bonds.

Build robust systems for tracking and reporting impact. According to ICMA guidelines, GSS+ bond issuers are expected to commit to timely and complete impact reporting. While local capacities for

[45] Environmental Finance. 2018. Green Bond Awards Winners. https://www.environmental-finance.com/content/awards/greenbond-awards-2018/winners/green-bond-of-the-year-local-authority-city-of-cape-town.html; City of Cape Town. 2023. CapeTown Announced as Leading African City for Climate Action. News release. 16 November. https://www.capetown.gov.za/Mediaand-news/Cape%20Town%20announced%20as%20leading%20African%20city%20for%20climate%20action.

measuring and reporting impact may vary, and some green and social project types may pose challenges for short-term quantification, it is essential that issuers disclose this information to maintain market integrity. Establishing internal impact data tracking systems not only supports compliance but can also enhance operational efficiency and governance, which are increasingly valued by sustainable investors.

4.4 Case Study 4. Île-de-France (France) Green and Sustainability Bonds

Table 10: Green and Sustainability Bonds in France's Capital Region

Standards Alignment External Review		
Pre-Issuance	Standards Alignment	ICMA Green Bond Principles (2021)
	External Review	Second-Party Opinion by Vigeo Eiris
Issuance (Recent)	Example ticker	IDF 2.9% 2031 (8y)
	Currencies	€ (euro)
	Details	91% of total outstanding debt was labeled green or sustainable as of end 2023
	Main Project Categories	Clean Transportation (70.6%)
Post-Issuance	Allocation Reporting	Green Buildings (19.7%), based on the 2023 allocation report
	Impact Reporting	Portfolio and project-level indicators
	Independent Auditing	Post-Issuance verification
	Accessible Disclosures	All framework documents, second-party opinions, and annual reports are available on the region's investor page

ICMA = International Capital Market Association.

Source: Authors' compilation based on Region Ile de France. Region Funding. https://www.iledefrance.fr/decouvrir-le-fonctionnement-de-la-region/region-funding.s

4.4.1 Issuer Background

Région Île-de-France is France's capital region, encompassing Paris and surrounding departments. It is the country's most populous region with 12.4 million residents, and an economic engine accounting for around 31% of national GDP. With GDP per capita of approximately 190% of the European Union (EU) average and over 1.2 million companies, Île-de-France is one of Europe's wealthiest and most dynamic territories.

The Regional Council has broad responsibilities including public transport, urban planning, high schools, economic development, and environmental policy. The region benefits from high credit ratings (Aa3/AA– in 2025), reflecting strong finances and support from the French state. This strong credit quality enabled it to become a pioneer in sustainable finance: in 2012, Île-de-France was the first local authority in Europe to issue a green bond.

4.4.2 Local Challenges and Issuer Motivation

Île-de-France faces significant sustainability challenges in transport emissions, aging public buildings, and social disparities. In 2016, the regional administration declared the fight against climate change a core priority, adopting an ambitious environmental road map. This was followed with multiple thematic initiatives including a clean air plan; a regional circular economy strategy; the Biodiversity Plan, 2020–2030; and sector plans for solar, hydrogen, methanization, and bicycling to drive emissions reductions and ecosystem protection.

The motivation to issue GSS+ bonds arose from a desire to align the region's financing with its policy goals. GSS+ bonds provide a way to raise long-term funds for transit expansions, energy-efficient buildings, and social projects. In 2019, the region made a landmark decision to finance 100% of its new borrowing through green or sustainable debt.

4.4.3 GSS+ Financing Framework Development and Issuance Approach

Île-de-France launched its first green bond in 2012, ahead of formal market standards. Its framework was then gradually aligned with the ICMA Green and Social Bond Principles, and in 2021 it was updated into a unified Green, Social, and Sustainability Bond Framework. This framework maps eligible projects to the United Nations Sustainable Development Goals and EU Taxonomy criteria. A Sustainable Finance Committee oversees project selection and ensures that proceeds are tracked, allocated, and reported annually.

The framework covers both environmental and social categories: low-carbon transport, energy-efficient schools and buildings, renewable energy, biodiversity, education, affordable housing, health, and economic inclusion (**Table 11**). This range allows the region to fund its core climate priorities while retaining flexibility to respond to social needs, as seen in 2020 when part of an €800 million ($702 million equivalent) bond was allocated to COVID-19 health and recovery measures. Project expenditures are certified by the regional public finance directorate, adding an independent control layer.

Table 11: Île-de-France's Green and Sustainable Financing Framework

Eligible Categories	Primary Type	Sample Projects	Impact Indicators	SDG Alignment
Green Buildings	Mitigation	Construction of energy efficient public buildings, school facilities, and public housing	CO_2 emissions avoided (tCO_2e/year); Number of project beneficiaries; Full-time equivalent jobs generated	11, 13
Clean Transportation	Mitigation	Construction of rail transport infrastructure and associated subsystems; construction of low-carbon road transport infrastructure dedicated to public passenger transport		9, 11, 13
Renewable Energy	Mitigation	Projects contributing to local renewable energy generation and energy efficiency		7, 12, 13
Terrestrial and Aquatic Biodiversity Conservation	Environment	Restoration and rehabilitation of ecosystems, sustainable forest management, investment in protected areas		6, 15
Access to Essential Services: Education	Social	Providing access to quality education through construction of additional educational accommodation capacity, and improvements to existing infrastructure		4, 8, 10
Access to Essential Services: Health	Social	Projects contributing to the development of health infrastructure and the purchase of health-care equipment; Projects related to health research and development		3, 11
Access to Essential Services: Social Inclusion	Social	Development of accommodative capacity for vulnerable populations; Projects to make buildings and infrastructure more accessible to people with reduced mobility		4, 10, 11
Affordable Housing	Social	Projects to develop and renovate the social housing stock, in line with environmental and social requirements		1, 11
Affordable Basic Infrastructure	Social	Development of transport, energy, green space, and sports infrastructure for better access to the entire territory, improved comfort, safety, and accessibility, etc.		8, 11
Support for Employment Creation and SME Financing	Social	Projects contributing to the creation or maintenance of employment via support for SMEs		1, 8

SDG = Sustainable Development Goal, SMEs = small and medium-sized enterprises, tCO_2e = tons of carbon dioxide equivalent.
Source: Authors' compilation.

Île-de-France has become a regular issuer, coming to market nearly every year with €500 million–€800 million transactions. The program has scaled up steadily from the inaugural €350 million issue in 2012 to annual issuance amounts of €800 million–€1.0 billion in recent years, cumulatively raising over €7.6 billion by 2025 (**Figure 15**). Strong demand has allowed the region to price inside its conventional yield curve and diversify its investor base across Europe. This consistent issuance strategy, paired with transparent annual impact reporting, has established the region as one of Europe's leading sub-sovereign sustainable bond issuers. The program's credibility is evidenced by external recognition: In 2021, the region was awarded "Best Sustainable Bond Issuer–France" by Capital Finance International for its €800 million COVID-19 response bond, and in 2023 it received Environmental Finance's award for local authority bond of the year.

Figure 15: Evolution of Île-de-France's GSS+ Bond Issuance (€ million)

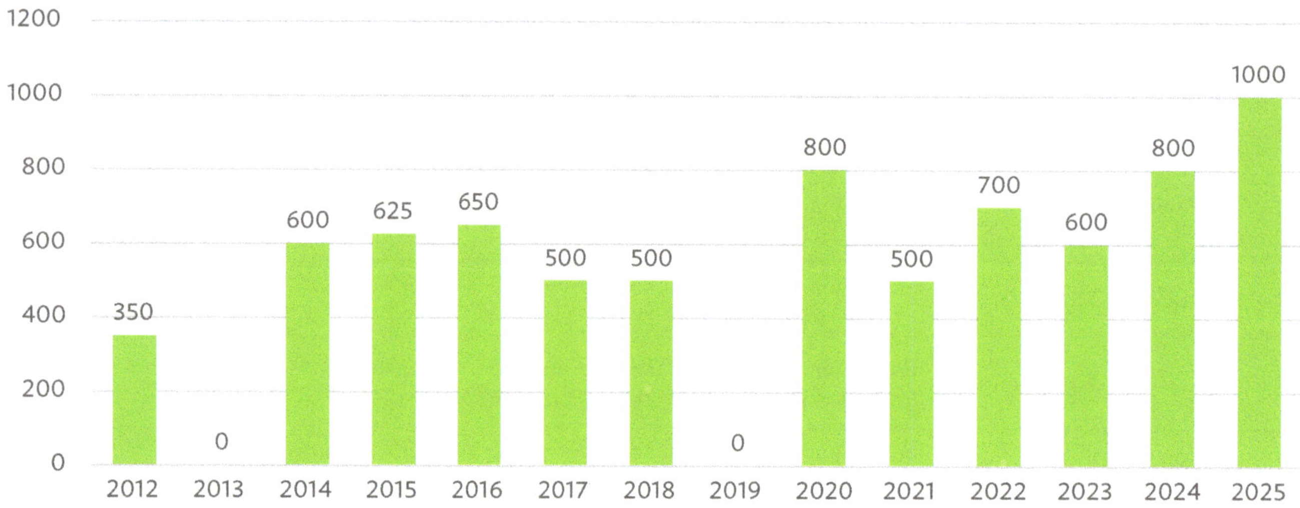

GSS+ = green, social, sustainability, sustainability-linked, and other labeled bonds.

Authors' compilation based on Region Ile de France. Region Funding. https://www.iledefrance.fr/decouvrir-le-fonctionnement-de-la-region/regionfunding.

4.4.4 GSS+ Project Allocations and Impact Reporting

Proceeds from Île-de-France's GSS+ bonds are mainly directed to clean transport and green buildings, reflecting the region's largest climate challenges. In 2023, 70% of the €600 million bond financed metro, tram, and rail projects, while about 20% was allocated to the construction and renovation of energy-efficient schools (**Figure 16**). Other project allocations include renewable energy networks (about 1%) and social categories such as education facilities, affordable housing, and community infrastructure (about 9% combined).

Figure 16: Île-de-France—Green and Sustainable Bond Project Allocations in 2023

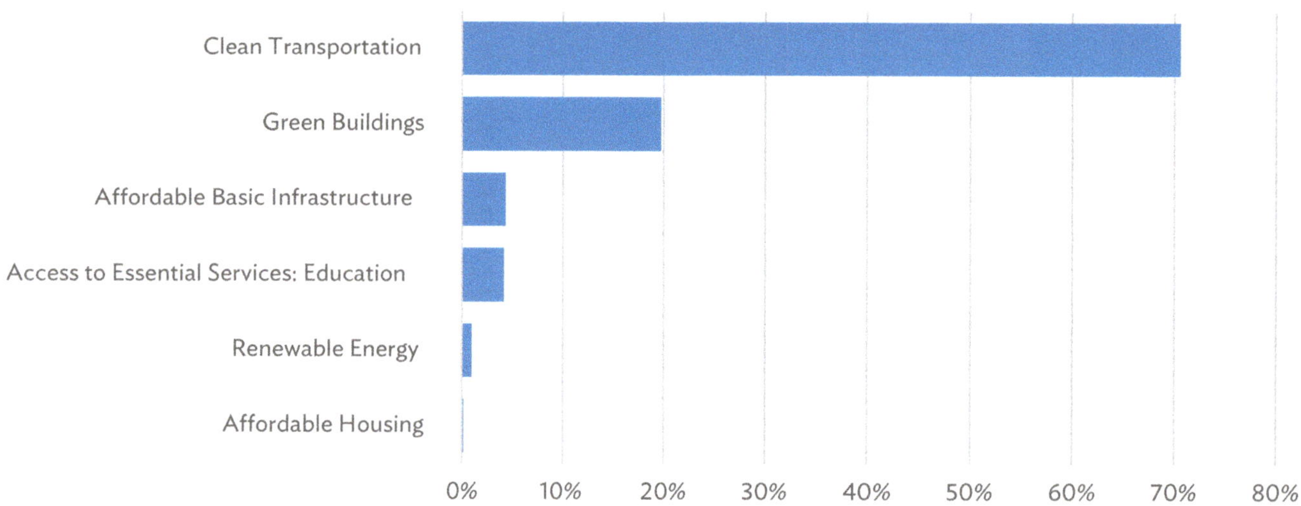

Source: Authors' calculations based on issuer sustainable financing framework and Region Ile de France 2023 Report.

Figure 17: Project Allocation Breakdown for GSS+ Bonds

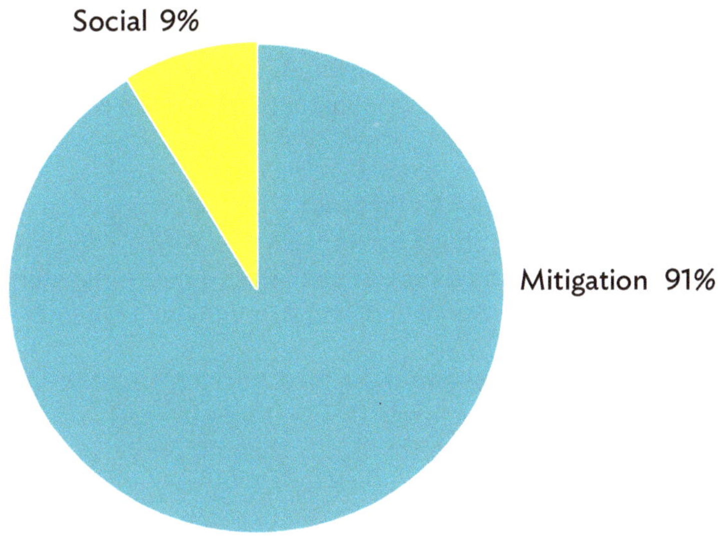

GSS+ = green, social, sustainability, sustainability-linked, and other labeled bonds.
Source: Authors' calculations based on issuer sustainable financing framework and Region Ile de France 2023 Report.

The region publishes annual allocation and impact reports in French and English. These detail how funds are spent and present indicators such as length of new transit lines, carbon emissions avoided, the energy performance of schools, and numbers of students or housing units supported. Methodologies are disclosed, and reporting is assured by external auditors.

Impact reporting is supplemented with case studies of flagship projects. For example, the Réseau Express Régional line E network (RER) rail network extension is expected to cut thousands of daily car trips, while geothermal networks rely on renewable energy to provide heat to households.

4.4.5 Assessment and Key Outcomes

Since 2012, Île-de-France has issued over €7.6 billion in green and sustainability bonds, resulting in 92% of its debt stock being sustainable in 2024. This financing has enabled major investments, primarily in climate mitigation projects such as low-carbon transport and energy-efficient schools, alongside targeted social projects such as student housing and small and medium-sized support during the COVID-19 pandemic (**Figure 17**). Regular issuance has diversified the investor base, attracted strong international demand (e.g., the 2023 bond was nearly fourfold oversubscribed and attracted 94 investors from 15 countries), and delivered financing at competitive spreads, reinforcing the region's financial resilience.

Beyond financing, the program has strengthened governance and transparency. Annual allocation and impact reports, external reviews, and project case studies have built strong investor confidence and public accountability. Awards and top ESG ratings reflect the credibility of this approach. The main gap has been limited funding for adaptation, but new plans on resilience and green budgeting suggest future issuances will increasingly cover these needs.

4.4.6 Key Lessons Learned

Make sustainable finance the default. Île-de-France's decision to issue only green and sustainability bonds since 2019 ensured that every new borrowing supported its climate and social agenda. This clear commitment simplified communication with investors and created predictability in the pipeline, which in turn helped build credibility.

Strong frameworks and transparency build trust. The region regularly updates its GSS+ framework to align with evolving standards such as the EU Taxonomy and ICMA Principles. Annual allocation and impact reports, external assurance, and detailed project indicators provide investors with reliable evidence of impact, reducing concerns about greenwashing and strengthening long-term market confidence.

Leadership and coordination are essential. Political backing from the Regional Council and the creation of the Sustainable Finance Committee allows the bond program to cut across departments and integrate climate, transport, education, and social priorities. This coordination guarantees a robust and diversified pipeline of eligible projects that could be financed consistently year after year.

Consistency strengthens market access. By issuing almost every year, the region built a strong track record and established itself as a reference issuer among sub-sovereigns. This regular presence in the market attracted international investors, generated oversubscriptions, and allowed the region to tighten spreads compared to conventional bonds.

5. Recommendations

Mobilizing and scaling up sustainable finance for local governments is a common challenge across developing economies in Asia and the Pacific. Addressing this effectively requires a coordinated and multilayered policy approach across levels of government. While there is no single "right approach," mechanisms and frameworks established in other contexts to develop efficient local government financing markets can serve as valuable reference points for Asia and Pacific policymakers.

The following recommendations summarize the key findings of this paper and outline practical steps for establishing market-based local government financing, with a focus on mobilizing capital for municipal projects that deliver positive economic, environmental, and social outcomes:

1. **Align local government project financing with sovereign sustainable financing frameworks.** Local governments are primary providers of public investment and urban infrastructure for climate and social needs. However, they often lack the financial resources and borrowing capability to effectively deliver on these demands. Central government policymakers can advance national development priorities by enabling responsible municipal borrowing that addresses sustainability challenges at the local level. They can also promote the development of local sustainable investment project pipelines by providing guidance through their own sovereign sustainable financing frameworks.

2. **Establish pooled local government financing vehicles to scale local government bond markets, with a focus on green and social finance.** Pooled municipal financing vehicles are a proven approach for expanding subnational government access to capital by aggregating local issuance needs and consolidating resources into a single well-capitalized entity. These vehicles can lower borrowing costs, improve operational efficiency, and enhance market credibility through their scale, while also increasing market transparency and the functionality of municipal finance markets. in many cases, they become leaders in developing high-quality green and social public financing frameworks and in mainstreaming sustainability standards in their jurisdictions.

3. **Leverage multinational development bank resources and guarantees to kickstart local government bond markets.** Development finance organizations such as the Asian Development Bank can play a catalytic role in developing municipal finance markets though both financial support and technical assistance. Examples of such support can include initial capital contributions, partial credit guarantees, and technical support for developing subnational borrowing frameworks and preparing project pipelines

4. **Strengthen financial oversight, disclosure, and governance frameworks for sustainable local government financing, including those based on green and social taxonomies**. Reassuring investors that local-government-financed projects are backed by a secure and reliable repayment structure is critical for developing trust and securing market access for municipal issuers. But local government borrowers must also demonstrate their own integrity and capacity for responsible fundraising through frameworks for financial and sustainability disclosure and high-quality governance. Issuing green, social, and sustainability bonds based on taxonomies and globally recognized frameworks such as the ICMA Green, Social, and Sustainability Bond Principles can significantly enhance the credibility and attractiveness of local government bonds to long-term investors.

6. Conclusion

The need for public investment in sustainable and resilient infrastructure at the subnational level is significant, yet funding from direct local tax revenues and central government grants and loans is often limited and short term. Developing local government capital markets through the issuance of GSS+ bonds can help local governments bridge these investment gaps with cost-efficient and long-term financing.

The need for channeling climate finance flows to adaptation and resilience projects along with mitigation efforts is urgent, as global climate action remains insufficient. At the same time, local governments are uniquely well positioned to develop pipelines of adaptation and resilience projects, generating a natural source of adaptation finance opportunities where private capital can invest.

Around the world, local governments such as Tokyo, Gothenburg, Cape Town, and Île-de-France have successfully leveraged GSS+ bond issuance to meet their diverse climate investment needs, deepen local debt capital markets, and deliver long-term benefits from sustainable and resilient development for their citizens. Their pioneering approaches and the resulting lessons learned offer practical lessons for other subnational entities to develop their own GSS+ local government bond programs in Asia and the Pacific.

www.ingramcontent.com/pod-product-compliance
Lightning Source LLC
Chambersburg PA
CBHW041759220926
51847CB00014B/260
* 9 7 8 9 2 9 2 7 7 5 6 1 2 *